The Cheese Room

The Cheese Room

PATRICIA MICHELSON

MICHAEL JOSEPH
an imprint of
PENGUIN BOOKS

MICHAEL JOSEPH
Published by the Penguin Group
Penguin Books Ltd, 80 Strand, London WC2R 0RL, England
Penguin Putnam Inc., 375 Hudson Street, New York, New York 10014, USA
Penguin Books Australia Ltd, 250 Camberwell Road, Camberwell, Victoria 3124, Australia
Penguin Books Canada Ltd, 10 Alcorn Avenue, Toronto, Ontario, Canada M4V 3B2
Penguin Books India (P) Ltd, 11 Community Centre, Panchsheel Park, New Delhi – 110 017, India
Penguin Books (NZ) Ltd, Cnr Rosedale and Airborne Roads, Albany, Auckland, New Zealand
Penguin Books (South Africa) (Pty) Ltd, 24 Sturdee Avenue, Rosebank 2196, South Africa

Penguin Books Ltd, Registered Offices: 80 Strand, London WC2R 0RL, England

www.penguin.com
First published 2001
8

Set in 10.75/14.25 pt Adobe Caslon
Typeset by Rowland Phototypesetting Ltd,
Bury St Edmunds, Suffolk
Printed in England by Clays Ltd, St Ives plc

A CIP catalogue record for this book is available from the British Library

ISBN 0-718-14442-2

Dedicated with love to H.L.K.

CONTENTS

FOREWORD

This book was conceived and written in the white heat of a small thriving business, coping with the success of an idea that germinated several years ago. My wife Patricia never ceases to amaze me, our friends and family with her talent, knowledge and wisdom, not just about cheese but all things gastronomic. How she found the time and dedication to write while being a wife, mother, and the driving force behind La Fromagerie remains a mystery, and a source of inspiration to us all.

Daniel Michelson
March 2001

THE CHEESE ROOM

Every day I open the door to the Cheese Room and roll up the protective blinds to reveal my 'treasures', sitting on their aged wooden shelves on straw mats. And every day I learn a little more about cheese and how I can make them taste of their particular *terroir* rather than masking their flavours. At the end of the day as I stroll home across Highbury Fields I may see a pizza delivery scooter roar past me at full throttle, trying to reach its destination by the allotted time. I can't help thinking that when I get home I'll simply slice two thin pieces of sourdough bread, toast them lightly, brush over a fruity white wine, lay slivers of Gruyère on top of one slice and crumble a goat's cheese over the other. Then I'll grill them until they are golden and melting. Just eight minutes from start to finish. Fast food – my way.

INTRODUCTION

I could talk about cheese until the cows come home . . . describe the nuances and aromas, textures, styles and varying shades of yellow. I could list countless cheeses, with family histories, terrain formations and weather conditions, and enough data to make you glaze over and reach for the gin bottle. For those of you who are interested I have listed on page 203 my favoured reference books on cheese and others I have found illuminating and enjoyable. More to the point, I want this book to give you the urge to explore different cheeses and tastes from which you might previously have shied away because their aroma might have seemed too strong and gamey, or their names were so convoluted you were afraid to try to pronounce them or just plain scared to try anything new.

And it's not just tasting new cheeses, it's knowing how to use them in cooking or with other ingredients. I loathe the idea of mixing cheese into a mass of gunge just because I know it will melt or soften: the finished result will lose all the inherent texture and flavour of the cheese. Of course, there are certain cheeses, for example, the Gruyère style and crumbly Cheddars, which perform well when grilled or baked, and soft creamy cheeses that can be used in cake-baking, but generally I prefer to keep cheese intact to serve alongside other ingredients. I am not a chef, or a trained cook; so my recipe ideas are based first and foremost on making the most of cheese, with complementary seasonal produce. Whenever I'm visiting cheesemakers I love searching out local products, especially those that go well with cheese in one form or another. I love wine – it doesn't have to be massively expensive – and if a vineyard is near to where a cheese comes from, the two invariably match.

I love maturing and nurturing cheese, bringing out the best qualities of the milk. It can sometimes be a slow process, and requires a talent and skill rather like those of a winemaker. In Britain the number of cheesemongers practising these methods can be counted on the fingers of one hand – and I have named shops I consider worth a detour for really good cheese, mentioning those with maturing on site, on page 197. Also on my travels in Europe and the States I have found wonderful food shops, as well as meeting retailers who have visited my shop from Australia and New Zealand – and I have listed my favourites on pages 198–201, and some markets too, for you to search out.

I want to convey my enthusiasm and delight in discovering good cheese. I want you not only to beat a path to my shop, which would be lovely as I'll always be pleased to see you, but also to support your local cheesemonger or food shop and, if you live in a rural area, find artisan cheesemakers using milk from their own herd: knock at their door, and as likely as not they will be delighted to sell you their cheese, or tell you where to buy it. Farmers' markets are popping up everywhere, especially in cities and major towns, and should be assiduously patronized by all who value the importance of fresh, locally grown and reared produce. It doesn't have to be rigidly organic but should be grown or reared with care, patience and respect. If you find any good ones please let me know!

Let's also rediscover the joy and satisfaction of food shopping instead of relying solely on supermarkets. Think about menu planning each day instead of once a week when you do the main shopping. Look at simple foods like cheese and realize their potential in all sorts of recipes as well as being a complete meal with a chunk of bread, some olives, pickles and a glass of wine. What could be easier or more delicious?

My philosophy in cooking is to use really good ingredients and not twist them about, losing texture, aroma and flavour. We are learning more and more about produce being grown without too many chemicals, or indeed any manufactured aids, as well as enjoying the seasonality of food rather than expecting to see strawberries and asparagus all the year round. The same principles apply to cheese – look forward to new flavours as the seasons change.

Here are some personal thoughts on food and shopping. You don't have to take them as gospel, just as a guideline.

Wherever you can buy fruit, vegetables, salads, herbs as fresh as possible and look for produce that hasn't been oversprayed or over-cultivated. Ask your greengrocer, butcher, baker, fishmonger about their foods.

When it comes to butter, I prefer to use the French Charente butter as it is lighter and 'sweeter' than that from Normandy and makes lovely crisp pastry, as well as bases for soups, eggs, flavoured butters and cakes. I use bottled spring water, either plain or sparkling depending on what I am cooking (I cook lentils and dried beans in sparkling water, which makes them much tastier and less likely to fall apart). If you have a water purifier all the better: I live in London where the water is very hard and I find it just doesn't do the job when I'm making pastry or soups. This may sound quirky, but I am convinced that city dwellers do have different-tasting tap water from those who live in the country. In any event, try using tap water and then do the same recipe with spring water, and see if you notice the difference.

The eggs I prefer are free-range organic: I am really fussy about the hens' feed and whether they have enough daylight access to roam. I couldn't eat eggs for years because I used to have an allergic reaction to them and it was only when I started my business that I found eggs that liked me as much as I liked them. Salt should be organic sea salt – you'll use less and it tastes better. Pepper can be ground from a mill, but I like to use a pestle and mortar.

Meat should have that rich ruby colour rather than scarlet. You want it to have had a bit of time to mature, or 'hang', otherwise the taste will not be as juicy and the texture will be tough. The fat should be marbled evenly throughout and your butcher should be able to advise you, especially if he is a member of the Q Guild of Butchers. When it comes to buying chicken I have, in the past, found kosher chickens the tastiest as the methods of rearing and slaughter have to follow strict cultural rules and regulations. Lately, though, in the farmers' markets, I have purchased cracking good organic chickens that have been allowed to roam freely, ensuring a fleshy full-flavoured juicy bird. Their appearance is quite different from mass-produced specimens: natural and healthy rather than anaemic-looking and plumped up with goodness knows what. But it's the taste that is such a revelation: meaty, tender, a little hint of game – simply delicious.

As far as fish is concerned, the smell tells you all and the glistening gelatinous eyes and sparkling skin convince you. Use fish as soon as possible, although Dover sole may be better after a day or two in the fridge.

Don't use your finest extra-virgin olive oil for cooking, but a decent all-rounder. Save the best for drizzling over food or into soups: the better the oil, the better the taste. As for pulses and grains, see my notes in the Fava Bean and Chick Pea Soup recipe on page 83.

You will notice that not all the recipes include cheese as an ingredient. This is not because I ran out of ideas, but because I wanted also to put together food combinations that were complementary to cheese or fresh home-made cheeses. And they should all work, but if they aren't exactly right for you then modify them to your preferred methods – these recipes are not written on tablets of stone!

A GUIDELINE ON CHEESE MAINTENANCE

◆ Refreshing Cheeses
Before serving, refresh hard cheeses by scraping lightly with a sharp knife on the exposed side, removing any dried or slightly discoloured surfaces. Soft cheeses can also be scraped with a knife as necessary and any dry areas cut away. Remember to wash the knife in very hot water and dry with paper towel rather than a tea-towel after treating each cheese.

◆ Storage
All cut hard cheeses should have a smooth wrapping of clingfilm to protect their edge, leaving the crust to breathe naturally. This should be replaced each time the cheese is unwrapped.

All bloomy-crust cheeses should be wrapped in foil or waxed paper.

All blue cheeses should be wrapped in foil, or first in waxed paper and then foil if they are crumbly.

All washed-rind cheeses should be wrapped in waxed paper and then foil. Cheeses such as Époisses should always be sticky, but if you find your uncut cheese has dried out after a few days in the fridge, mix a little white wine with boiled and cooled water, then with your fingertips – which should be scrupulously clean – rub the liquid into the cheese until it feels slightly moist.

All goat's cheeses should be put on a plate with a food bag loosely covering them, or you can sit the cheeses side by side in a Tupperware-style container with a close-fitting lid.

For storage in the fridge cheese should be arranged on a tray with a clean damp tea-towel draped over it.

Before serving, take cheese out of the fridge and uncover it. It can then be placed on a cheeseboard, and covered with a clean barely damp tea-towel until it is taken into the dining room.

Remember: uncovered cheeses must never be placed in the fridge with other raw foods as they are easily tainted and spoilt.

WHY CHEESES TAKE ON DIFFERENT APPEARANCES

The introduction of moulds and the washing and curing of rinds change the way cheeses look. Most of the bacteria and micro-organisms are removed from pasteurized-milk cheeses by heating the milk to a certain point, so bacteria is introduced to the outside of the cheese to promote the growth of moulds to create bloomy or washed rinds. However, the overall taste of the cheese does not progress as would be the case if using unpasteurized (untreated) milk, from which the bacteria have not been extracted. If cheese is kept in a too-humid environment or is allowed to dry out too quickly, the flavours are unrewarding. However, cheese made with unpasteurized milk and allowed to ripen and mature at its own pace, developing tastes and textures of complexity and length, will retain all of the inherent quality of the milk. All natural products contain a multitude of bacteria, some good some bad, but with careful preparation and hygiene in all areas of the dairy the bad ones will be eliminated by the good ones during the ripening process. It is worth noting that sloppy methods produce tainted results in pasteurized as well as unpasteurized milk cheeses.

With softer creamy cheeses, unless they are to be sold very fresh indeed – for example, Petits Suisses – a mould is introduced to the outside, called *Penicillium candidum*. It is a natural microbe present in the air and the cheese develops a bloomy white coat. This mould develops naturally on unpasteurized milk cheeses. You can tell when a rind has been artificially introduced as it will appear rather thick and almost detached from the cheese: you can peel it off, rather as you would an orange. A raw milk cheese will have a thin layer of perfectly formed soft white velvety mould, which adheres to it.

Soft-textured cheeses, like Époisses and Ami Chambertin, have *Penicillium linum* on the rind after they are salted then washed in a salt-water brine or wine or other alcohol. The glistening orange appearance develops in cool cellars with high humidity. Some cheeses, such as Reblochon from the Savoie or Celtic Promise from Britain, develop a rind that is smoothed, brushed and carefully rubbed in a brine solution to give an apricot/peach appearance: it is not sticky but supple.

Blue cheeses are produced when *Penicillium glaucum* is introduced via needles, which aerate the cheese allowing the mould to penetrate into the interior. *Penicillium roqueforti* gives Roquefort the character and style that distinguishes it from other blue cheeses. This method is used for all blue cheeses. However, the artisan-made ones have time to develop their moulds at a slower pace, and the blue veins generally appear more evenly spread throughout the cheese.

Why do cheeses take on strong, pungent odours? The rinds, especially washed ones, react to the natural fermentation of the milk caused by the oxygen in the air. Now you may think this can be compared to old socks, smelly feet, or wet dog, but these earthy, rotting-leaf type aromas should be delicious: it is only when fermentation has been badly administered, or the milk has been tainted that the odours become aggressive and unpleasant. A good *affineur* (cheese-maturer) will take care to evolve the cheese to its natural conclusion – a state that is not only appealing to the eye, but also attractive to the nose and ultimately delicious in the mouth. A washed-rind cheese such as Époisses, Ami Chambertin, Munster,

Livarot or Maroilles will react adversely if kept wrapped in plastic and not allowed to develop in a natural environment.

It is just as easy to tell when hard cheeses have had too little care lavished on them: the holes in Emmental should not be too small or too large but even-sized and randomly distributed – avoid the ones with large, unevenly shaped holes. After the milk is heated to a temperature as high as 120°F, a starter is added, containing bacteria to produce carbon-dioxide gas. When the cheese is drained and shaped, it is placed in a humid maturing room. The holes are formed by internal 'explosions' as the cheese reacts to the atmosphere in the cellar.

Gruyère-style cheeses have a few small holes or little splits in the interior, and sometimes when you open a cheese it 'weeps', which is the salt melting through the cheese. This is good: it shows careful production, and the cheese will taste nutty, grainy with a sweet fruitiness.

Cheddar-style cheeses with a lot of interior cracking have either been dried out too quickly, or given too much rennet, or been otherwise badly handled through the various stages of production. A little blue running through a hard cheese, especially a farmhouse, cloth-wrapped or unpasteurized milk one, is not necessarily a bad thing – it is a natural product and the mould will add to the overall flavour.

CHEESE AND CONTROVERSY

There has been much publicity about health issues relating to food, but a government survey, conducted after a recent listeria outbreak, noted that dairy products were rarely responsible for food poisoning. Cheese was less likely to cause illness than water, and unpasteurized milk cheese was deemed even better. Of course, if cheese is responsible for a health scare this may be due to bad handling along the food chain rather than to the milk used in its production. Unpasteurized milk cheese has never been proved to be unsafe even though alarm bells are rung at every opportunity. Here is an excerpt from a paper by Dr B. M. Pickard of Leeds University, 'The Case for Untreated (Unpasteurized) Milk', which was first published by the Soil Association:

There is no doubt that heat treatment is detrimental to milk.

Evidence shows that untreated milk has a higher nutritional value, providing more available vitamins and minerals than pasteurized milk. It contains anti-infective agents which can both restrict the growth of contaminating bacteria in the milk and give the consumer protection. Not least, it has a better flavour, with none of the deterioration in quality caused by heat treatment.

Whilst it is eminently reasonable to stamp out any significant cause of disease and to penalize those whose conditions of hygiene are poor, it is unjust to suggest that all untreated milk should be pasteurized because of isolated outbreaks of infection whether or not they have been conclusively linked to untreated milk consumption.

The rational approach to hygiene is obviously necessary but it is nonsensical to hope for a situation in which our food is sterile.

It makes more sense to opt for the institution of a reasonable degree of hygiene combined with the promotion of vigorous good health and the associated resistance to disease which comes from eating natural wholesome foods which have not been unnecessarily processed.

Eighteen months ago, the Specialist Cheese Association decided, quite rightly, that the time had come to employ microbiologists and scientists to work alongside the Food Standards Agency and the Ministry of Agriculture, Fisheries and Food, so that dairy produce made with raw milk could be judged in a fair and ethical manner even though it only accounts for a tiny proportion of total production.

However, public reaction to media reporting has caused a loss of confidence in a vital primary food source. In 1997, after many conversations with customers in my shop who were pregnant and worried about the safety of cheese, I wrote a leaflet to attempt to reassure them. I reproduce it here, as I believe it bears witness to events since it was written, and highlights relevant issues. Of course, these are my own views, and you can either ignore them or mull them over and reach your own conclusion.

We have often been asked what cheeses can be eaten during pregnancy, and this leaflet outlines a few facts and suggestions to make your 'confinement' as enjoyable and food-fad-free as possible. The term eating for two doesn't mean doubling up on everything consumed during the nine months of pregnancy. What it should mean is thinking practically and confidently about the sort of foods consumed during the day that don't (a) give you indigestion and, (b) make you feel ill.

However, first it must be stated that changing eating habits as soon as you become pregnant is noble, but if you are thinking about starting a family, then concentrating on good and healthy eating should begin at least three months before you want to conceive. This enables your body to adjust to a new routine in readiness for the oncoming nine long months of pregnancy.

Thinking about what is good for your body does not need an Einstein brain. In fact so much is written in the media, both well researched and badly thought out, that eating habits become muddled and ideas unfocused. Let's, then, go back to basics.

We need protein, carbohydrates, vitamins and minerals, and these come from dairy foods, fish and meat products, cereals, vegetables and fruit. However, out of all these foods the cheese products have become an enemy to the pregnant woman. And this is because of the fear of listeria. Listeria hysteria has blown the issue out of all proportion and should be addressed: calcium from cheese makes strong teeth, bones and muscles. It is a vital ingredient for a healthy lifestyle.

Unpasteurized milk cheeses aren't out of bounds. Just think for a moment: if a cheese is made with untreated milk then both good and bad bacteria is in the cheese. However, the bacteria floating in the atmosphere that affect foods can be better combated when they land on unpasteurized milk cheeses where they are effectively zapped. The outside moulds on the cheeses are in effect 'God's Elastoplast' helping to protect and guard against any negative bacteria affecting the product. Also after nine plus months spent maturing, a hard cheese made with untreated milk is free of any problems making it perfectly suitable for anyone to eat.

On the question of soft, rinded cheeses and blue cheeses, again, cheeses made with treated milk are far more likely to cause problems than those made with unpasteurized milk. But the main factor with soft, rinded and washed cheeses is to take care especially with the bloomy crust, which should be cut away before eating. The rind is not only soft, but moist, a good breeding ground for *Listeria*. With pasteurized milk the bacteria grow fast and furiously, but with unpasteurized milk they are attacked and kept at bay, making the cheese less likely to cause upsets. With blue-veined cheeses you have to remember that mould is introduced into the entire cheese, which makes for a much longer digesting process with the richer and more complex mixtures of bacteria and fats, and they should be avoided in large amounts by pregnant women. However, in small quantities they can be mixed with light, fresh ricotta-type cheeses and used as, say, stuffings for pancakes, for an easy lunch.

It may also be worth noting that by cutting away the soft bloomy rind you are effectively cutting the fat content of the cheese in half, as this is the part of the cheese that contains the highest percentage of fat. As softer creamier cheeses take longer to digest, they should be eaten earlier in the day rather than in the evening. In fact, eating patterns during pregnancy should be carefully planned along the lines of cereals, fruit, weak tea or coffee, and plain yoghurt at breakfast; lunch should consist of a protein with salad or green vegetables, bread with plenty of natural roughage, and fruit. Tea breaks can consist of a biscuit or two and chocolate treats, or a selection of dried fruits, and dinner should be a lighter meal with perhaps a glass of wine to help you relax as well as aiding digestion.

A meal of cheese, good bread, salad dressed with a walnut or good olive oil (no vinegar), fresh or cooked fruits in all sorts of forms, a glass of red wine or clear apple or grape juice is a delightful way to enjoy not only your pregnancy but to embrace a good lifestyle.

The next question you should be addressing is how organic is the food you are eating? Chemicals, industrial fertilizers, animal feeds and methods of slaughter should all be issues investigated, improved and given prime consideration, especially by the supermarket giants churning out our everyday foodstuffs.

Since I wrote the leaflet the organic issue has been constantly in the press. People are becoming 'organi-maniacs', insisting that everything that passes their lips has been certified organic, but they are missing the point. Some of the cheeses I buy are from small, remote cheesemaking communities where traditional methods have been handed down the generations. Animals graze on high pastures, studded with alpine flora growing in clean mountain air. Fertilizers are natural. The farmers have no need of a stamp of certification on their product, and in any case they could not afford to refurbish their cheesemaking procedures to bring them into line with current modern techniques. I nurture them, am grateful for their produce and thankful for every cheese I receive in my shop as so few are made.

Taking care in rearing and feeding, with soil and pasture fertilizing, is just as important as eating organically produced food. What I want to see is care and commitment to every single element of our well-being from the soil to the table, for everyone and not just the lucky few who can afford to pay. Let's try to make the air we breathe, the rain that falls, the commitment to a healthy lifestyle something to which we all contribute.

A FEW WORDS ABOUT *AFFINAGE* – OR CHEESE-MATURING

Cheese is a simple food made more interesting by a knowledgeable *affineur*. Just as a good hairdresser can reshape your hair, making you feel like a million dollars, a cheese-maturer can tell by touch how a cheese is progressing, if another brine-washing is needed for the rind, or whether it is ready for eating.

The hands of an experienced *affineur* – at La Fromagerie our Merlin is Eric Demelle – can turn a mundane-tasting cheese into a full, fruity, fragrant morsel. They take an essentially modest food to its ultimate tasting power. There are clear rules in *affinage* but ultimately it is the *affineur*'s individuality in developing the taste and style of a cheese – their imprint – that creates the impact of flavours that, in some cases, spell out their name. For instance, our particular style is sufficiently evolved to be recognized by customers dining in restaurants where our cheeses appear unlabelled. This is praise indeed. It takes years for an *affineur* to fine-tune their craft, where the final outcome or destiny of the cheese is defined using olfactory terms (aromatic nuances, floral, fruity, earthy etc.), aspect (the overall look of the cheese), aromatic persistency (the pungency of both the crust and the inside of the cheese), flavours (whether the strength or milder qualities are coming through) to the end result (a cheese that is ripe and ready for eating).

As soon as the cheeses arrive at my shop we inspect them one by one, handling the soft ones gently to work out how they will develop. How plump and buttery the rind feels gives us an idea of how long the maturing process will take, and where in the maturing room we will store it, whether we want to hold it back a bit or bring it forward. The main purpose is to transform the cheese from its youth to a mature ripe state for perfect eating. Getting the ambient temperature of the maturing room right is paramount: it should be cool with a constant humidity of 85–95 per cent. Of course, a room below ground level is best, as it is quiet and still; a good atmosphere for cheese to ripen.

Having our own maturing rooms in the basement of the shop enables us to prepare the cheeses for greater taste impact. The quiet dark areas with perfect dampness and cooling units are fitted with aged shelving from a disused Cheddar storage barn in Somerset. Anyone else would have used it as firewood on Guy Fawkes' Night, but these fifty-year-old shelves are seasoned and happy to lie in this atmosphere. A hot-water scrub cleans them: we never use cleaning products down here as the natural flora would be destroyed and the bacterial balance would be upset. Then harmful bugs would place themselves on our delicate white moulds and show up as ugly black spots.

Soft cheeses, such as Époisses, will be sprayed with alcohol (ideally from the region where the cheese was produced) to help them become creamier and develop the rind, giving a fuller flavour. Eric won't let on exactly what he does, but when I rub a little wine-laced wash into the soft smooth rind of, say, a Reblochon from the alpine region of Savoie, to which I have also added a little *crème fraîche*, I gently massage the whole cheese with my fingertips so it is absorbed right the way through. In a week the texture will be supple, the rind will have taken on a beautiful apricot glow and the taste will be more nutty with a light fruity tang.

Once a cheese has been washed – or brushed if a hard rind is required – it is placed on a wooden shelf lined with mats made of natural, untreated straw, which I bring in from France. Then the *affineur* turns the cheeses so that they mature evenly; by constant observation he or she can see how the cheese is responding to the environment of the room.

Seasons play a part in the maturing process too. The quality of the milk changes from summer to winter. Cheeses taste quite sharp and strident when they have been made from winter milk when the cattle have less access to outside grazing and rely heavily on hay. In summer, they have a floral fragrance and rich taste because the cattle graze in warm meadows and pastures. Autumn cheeses are richest in texture, and the Vacherin Mont d'Or is in season only from October to March.

The Affineur's Choice for a cheeseboard would consist of five cheeses: goat, bloomy white crust, hard, washed and blue. However, one cheese such as the rich and creamy Vacherin Mont d'Or or a particularly nutty farmhouse Cheddar or a stunning three-year-old Parmigiano Reggiano needs no other partners, except, of course, a glass of wine – preferably not too overpowering. A fish main course might be followed by goat's cheeses; poultry, by medium-strength creamy cheeses; pasta, by sheep's milk Pecorino-type cheeses; beef or game, by washed-rind cheeses and blue cheeses; lamb, by Gruyère-style and crumbly English cheeses; rich stews, by sharp, crumbly cheeses. Main courses with creamy or full-flavoured wine sauces might be followed by supple-textured monastery-style cheeses.

GETTING ROUND THE PROBLEM OF ORDERING CHEESE IN RESTAURANTS

This is rather controversial, but I think it's about time somebody put the record straight. I'm afraid, when it comes to the cheese course, British restaurants have much to learn. For the few who make the effort to promote and display a decent selection of seasonal cheeses, with a member of staff willing and able to take charge of the cheeseboard, there are dozens of others who are lazy, ill-informed, careless and unable to grasp the fact that a good cheese selection shows how careful they are with sourcing their produce in general. This part of the menu has to rely on good suppliers rather than the skill of the kitchen staff. If a Michelin-starred chef can only rustle up plated cheese, he or she isn't doing their job properly.

If a restaurant serves only plated cheese, ask what is being offered. When it is placed before you, ask the waiter to indicate which cheese is which, and ask him or her for information about them. If they don't know, the wine waiter should, and do complain if you think the cheese is too cold, too old or badly kept.

If an otherwise good restaurant does not offer a cheese course, ask them why. A decent cheeseboard may help sell more wine, and there is no valid excuse about cheese (a) not being viable, or (b) no one asks for it.

When a restaurant's cheeseboard is presented to you, ask about the cheeses and their tasting styles. Make a point of finding out where they are from, what the milk type is, and whether they are aged or fresh. For a good rounded selection choose one hard, one soft bloomy crust, one creamy washed rind (light or fruity), one goat, one blue and, if you are allowed one more, try something with a herb or flavoured coating. If an Italian restaurant has a particularly good Parmigiano Reggiano, then order it with a side salad, or in the autumn with new season's walnuts. If you are in a French restaurant the cheeseboard will nearly always rely on French cheeses, unless the chef wants to highlight certain British cheeses that work well alongside their Gallic counterparts. British cheeses are firmly on the map now, and a restaurateur who serves only British cheese must ensure it is in tip-top form and that a good range is on offer. A good British cheese course is worth a detour, preferably eaten after dessert.

It's rather friendly to share a plate of cheese if you are dining out with friends. I think more restaurants should latch on to this idea: by the time you have arrived at this stage in the meal you are agreeably mellow and a little bit of nibbling and passing round of tasty morsels is, well, a sensuous interlude before dessert or coffee.

CONVERSION TABLES

WEIGHTS

7.5 g	¼ oz	85 g	3 oz	340 g	12 oz	1.1 kg	2½ lb
15 g	½ oz	100 g	3½ oz	370 g	13 oz	1.4 kg	3 lb
20 g	¾ oz	115 g	4 oz	400 g	14 oz	1.5 kg	3½ lb
30 g	1 oz	140 g	5 oz	425 g	15 oz	1.8 kg	4 lb
35 g	1¼ oz	170 g	6 oz	455 g	1 lb	2 kg	4½ lb
40 g	1½ oz	200 g	7 oz	565 g	1¼ lb	2.3 kg	5 lb
50 g	1¾ oz	225 g	8 oz	680 g	1½ lb	2.7 kg	6 lb
55 g	2 oz	255 g	9 oz	795 g	1¾ lb	3.1 kg	7 lb
65 g	2¼ oz	285 g	10 oz	905 g	2 lb	3.6 kg	8 lb
70 g	2½ oz	310 g	11 oz	1 kg	2 lb	4.5 kg	10 lb
80 g	2¾ oz				3 oz		

OVEN TEMPERATURES

Very cool	110°C	225°F	Gas ¼
Very cool	130°C	250°F	Gas ½
Cool	140°C	275°F	Gas 1
Slow	150°C	300°F	Gas 2
Moderately slow	170°C	325°F	Gas 3
Moderate	180°C	350°F	Gas 4
Moderately hot	190°C	375°F	Gas 5
Hot	200°C	400°F	Gas 6
Very hot	220°C	425°F	Gas 7
Very hot	230°C	450°F	Gas 8
Hottest	240°C	475°F	Gas 9

VOLUME

ml	fl oz		ml	fl oz	pint
5 ml		1 teaspoon	120 ml		
10 ml		1 dessertspoon	130 ml	4.5 fl oz	
15 ml	0.5 fl oz	1 tablespoon	140 ml	5 fl oz	¼ pint
20 ml			155 ml	5.5 fl oz	
25 ml			170 ml	6 fl oz	
30 ml	1 fl oz		180 ml		
35 ml			185 ml	6.5 fl oz	
40 ml	1.5 fl oz		200 ml	7 fl oz	
45 ml			215 ml	7.5 fl oz	
50 ml			225 ml	8 fl oz	
55 ml	2 fl oz		240 ml	8.5 fl oz	
60 ml			255 ml	9 fl oz	
70 ml	2.5 fl oz		270 ml	9.5 fl oz	
75 ml			285 ml	10 fl oz	½ pint
80 ml			315 ml	11 fl oz	
85 ml	3 fl oz		400 ml	14 fl oz	
90 ml	3.5 fl oz		425 ml	15 fl oz	¾ pint
95 ml			565 ml	20 fl oz	1 pint
100 ml			710 ml	25 fl oz	1¼ pints
105 ml			850 ml	30 fl oz	1½ pints
115 ml	4 fl oz		1 litre	35 fl oz	1¾ pints

CHEESES FOR ALL SEASONS

THE FIRST TASTE OF AUTUMN

The first true taste of autumn for me comes when the cheese table in my shop displays Vacherin Mont d'Or. Not for me the bland taste of early September cheeses: I prefer to wait until the end of October – or the weekend when we turn back the clocks in Britain – until the most seductive and sensual of cheeses is available.

To set the scene, understand the cheese ... The milk is rich and buttery, from the Montbéliarde cattle – hardy creatures used to roaming mountain pastures in the Haut Doubs region of France. In summer they move to high-mountain grazing to enjoy the lush herb and flower-strewn pastures and fresh clean mountain air. Next time you go skiing look out for the weathered faces of the lift operators: they are, more often than not, the herdsmen who look after the cattle in summer; in the winter months they make money 'herding' ski-mad tourists on to the lifts.

At the end of August the cattle are led down to the lower valleys, which are still warm and lush from the summer. They are in good humour, relaxed and producing an abundance of fine rich milk, which is transformed into voluptuous thick curds and placed in wooden moulds to settle. Then a strip of bark encircles each cheese to keep it intact and impart to it a sappy alpine flavour.

When the cheeses arrive at the shop we enhance the flavour by lightly washing the crust with a Jura or an Arbois white wine, mixed with boiled and cooled water, then leaving the cheeses to ripen in our cool cellars with high humidity. One of the reasons I called my business La Fromagerie was because I wanted to run it on the lines of the French cheese shops where *affinage* is an integral part of the service. We treat British, Italian, Irish, Spanish and Portuguese cheeses with the same care and attention to bring out their unique flavours. Sometimes we go a little too far – after all, we are dealing with a natural, living product – and the tastes go a bit wild but no matter: they are still interesting, if somewhat explosive, and we turn what many would consider simple yellow stuff into a full-flavoured complex confection.

The peachy crust on top of the Vacherin has a downy fluff, making it look like the folds of a satin peignoir, and the taste is a soft, silky, melting sensation. The velvet texture and sappy earthy taste is an experience to be shared, and keeps my spirits up during the cold dark months of winter.

With the smaller individually boxed cheeses, you can make a fondue.

Baked Vacherin

Wrap a small or medium boxed cheese in foil and place it on the middle shelf of your oven at 180°C/350°F/Gas Mark 4. Bake it for 20 minutes, then remove the foil and the lid of the box. Carefully cut out a circle around the crust and lift it off to reveal the cheese. Swirl in a little fruity white wine (not Chardonnay, rather a sauvignon blanc or, better still, a Savoie wine such as Chignin), and dip bite-sized steamed new potatoes into it. Serve it with a green salad dressed with walnut oil, thinly sliced charcuterie, tiny cornichons and maybe some tiny sweet and sour onions (see Braised Balsamic Onions, page 55). Don't be tempted to add any other ingredients to the cheese, such as herbs, as they will detract from its own flavour.

WINTER CHEESES – When Beaufort Met Patricia

I came to skiing rather late, but after the initial shock of constantly losing my balance and coming down the mountain on my backside rather than upright, I grew to love it. Especially when I was following ski instructors with their easy, cheeky style of shimmying down the runs. You use every muscle in your body and a tremendous amount of energy so by the end of the day you're really hungry. It was on a particular late afternoon after a strenuous pounding of the slopes that I was dragging myself through the village of Méribel back to the chalet and I was starving. I dropped into the local cheese shop and bought a small piece of Beaufort, the local cheese, to nibble on my way. The taste was so satisfying that I expect it was then I decided my life had to change: I wanted *everyone* to be able to enjoy this cheese. So, when it comes to cold winter days I think of Beaufort, with its rich, savoury fruitiness and grainy chewy texture. Just a small piece fills you up and makes you feel happy. I have fond memories of finding my original cheesemaker, Monsieur Jules Roux-Daigue, at the Moutiers Farmers' Market and lugging my first 35-kilo cheese home in the back of the car, both daughters wedged beside it and complaining about its pong. What struck me about Monsieur Roux-Daigue's cheeses was that they tasted like new season's hazelnuts – milky and nutty – with a sweet floral tang. He explained that his farm in Aiguebelle was in a sheltered part of the valley and the Tarentaise cows had quite an easy journey up to the *alpage*, high herb- and flower-strewn pastures, in the summer, so they were contented, well fed and not put under undue stress. His cheeses, all hand-made from scratch, developed their own identity, some with small cracks appearing in the cheese where the salt had dispersed, and some with maybe one or two tiny holes that gave character and charm to the finished cheese. Sadly he is no longer with us, but his reputation lingers on with each cheese I open just before Christmas – we save the special two-year forms for the end of the year.

In cold weather we need fuel food to keep us going, but it doesn't have to be boring. A plate of cheese at this time of the year serves as a restorative, and think of all the vitamins and proteins in it that ensure your body keeps healthy and strong.

Whether you use cheese in toasted snacks, or layered with potatoes and ham, or melted into fondue, it is essentially a complete food, a primary source of nourishment. Try to keep it separate from other foods: make cheese the main rather than the auxiliary part of what you are eating.

When children come home from school, have ready cubes of mild or medium-strong cheese with slices of apple for instant hunger relief. At breakfast, instead of a fry-up, thinly slice Mimolette Vieux, an orange-coloured hard cheese from Flanders with a taste not dissimilar to Gouda, and pile it on toasted buttered sourdough bread. A mild Gouda-type cheese is nourishing first thing in the morning or as an early lunch. If you look at one of Monet's paintings, *The Luncheon* (1868), you will see a table set for his meal – which was always timed for 11.30 a.m. – with a plate of sliced cheese, cold meats and soft-boiled eggs in the English style: he was very fond of English cheeses and especially the ritual of breakfast.

CHEESES FOR SPRING

First we have to decide when spring actually starts. Is it the beginning, middle or end of March? For me it's when the Vacherin Mont d'Or season finishes, towards the end of the month. By then I'm ready for refreshing goat's cheeses: sharp and tangy from the newly sprouted fresh grass and young stinging nettles topped with their pretty mauve flowers – a natural coagulant for the milk – that the animals are chewing. I have a theory about the character of milk: cows chew all day long, slowly digesting their food and producing a rich and buttery-textured milk. Sheep, with their small scissor-shaped teeth, neatly graze the top of the fleshy grass, leaving a wedge to shoot up new blades quickly; the animals are nervous but easily herded together, prefer comfort and routine, and their translucent milk tastes sweet and floral. Goats devour the grass right down to soil level; they are highly strung with a prickly temperament, searching out food high and low, and using up a lot of energy in the process. Their milk tastes sharp and sometimes aggressive, especially if they have been allowed to roam in hilly, rocky terrain. If a dairy keeps its goats indoors under controlled conditions, the milk tastes uniform and rather bland.

A tray of fresh goat's cheeses in all their different shapes and sizes – some with plain white bloomy moulds, some with a charcoal-ash coat, some covered with chestnut leaves – is a truly beautiful sight to behold. And the taste is a welcome respite from the heavier winter cheeses: it is a cheerful, lively herald of, hopefully, sunnier days and warm, balmy evenings. Tiny spring artichokes can be deep-fried in a light oil until golden and crisp, then served piping hot with a cold fresh moist goat's cheese crumbled over the top.

CHEESES FOR SUMMER

Can we ever rely on summer weather in England? Probably not . . . but there again I think it would be pretty boring if every day we could say, 'Well, it's another fabulous morning, isn't it?' Handsome is as handsome does, and I prefer my days to be unpredictable. Whether I'm picnicking with the warm breeze fluttering my hair, or cowering under a tree as the rain pelts down, as long as my basket of favourite food is safe, I'm happy.

Now you may think that cheeses for summer would be an oozing Brie, or a salad with mozzarella and tomatoes, but that is not always the case. In England we can enjoy the simple pleasure of a Guernsey milk cheese called Waterloo, with a rich buttery density and nutty taste, from cheese-makers Andy and Ann Wigmore, based in Riseley, Berkshire. I mature their cheeses for a few weeks until the thin white mould on the rind has wrinkled a little and turned a dusty biscuit grey. As you cut through the crust the interior is soft and melting, the centre slightly crumbly. The taste is rounded, nutty and interesting, and most agreeable with a tray of squeaky fresh baby carrots, celery, radishes and crisp home-baked Scottish oatcakes. The Salers Cantal cheese from the Auvergne is in complete contrast: like a Cheddar but with more fruit and nut flavours and, as it warms in the mouth, a definite tingle on the tongue. Served with a slightly chilled Beaujolais and crusty bread it's a great way to end the day and watch the sun set.

Cheese really comes into its own at this time of year, and it's so easy to prepare a feast based around it with bread, salad, fruit and wine or cider. Before you feel confident enough to mix and match, stick to a theme of, say, seven French, Italian or English varieties, with light to medium to strong flavours. When you are ready to experiment, start with an Explorateur, which is a rich, triple-cream cheese, a creamy white mould rind, such as Brie de Meaux or Brie de Melun, or Coulommiers, a supple-textured cheese, not too aged, in the style of St Nectaire, with its farmyard rustic aroma but smooth chewy texture. Include a goat's milk cheese with a coat of ash that somehow evens out the acidity, then turn your attention to something like a young, rich, creamy Gorgonzola *dolce cremificato*, and end with a mellow hard sheep's milk cheese, such as Berkswell from Coventry in the West Midlands, and a fresh, crumbly farmhouse Lancashire or Wensleydale, tasting of newly cut sweetly savoury meadow grass. Have a big basket of assorted bread, a dish of sea-salt crystals to sprinkle over the cheese, a salad dressed with walnut oil and walnut vinegar (or lemon juice), olives, baby gherkins and roasted shallots in balsamic vinaigrette.

To go with the very rich triple-cream cheeses, have ready a bowl of cherries and strawberries and use the fruit to scoop up the cheese. Or have a selection of fresh goat's cheeses, especially those from Provence, such as Banon, Pebre d'Ase and Sariette, to serve with hot, peppery salad leaves dressed with walnut or hazelnut oil. Whether you are putting together a selection for two or two hundred, this is a trouble-free, easy way of entertaining.

Light, salty cheeses, such as a real Greek feta made with goat's and sheep's milk, are refreshing in hot weather. Served cubed and tossed with roughly torn crunchy lettuce and sorrel leaves, chopped cucumber, stoned Kalamata olives, snipped chives and chervil, then dressed with a fruity olive oil and lemon juice, it is a treat to savour with its bright, perky, effervescent tastes. (Sorrel is really easy to grow, either in a pot or among the roses in your flower-bed. Prized for its sharp lemon tangy leaves, it works a treat with fresh creamy cheeses or chopped into *fromage frais* as a dip.)

At this time of year, experiment with cheeses you would normally eat matured: it opens up a whole new taste experience. Take a plump ripe fig or plum, split it (and stone a plum) then crumble over it the freshest possible Richard III Wensleydale – difficult to get, I know, but tell your cheesemonger that it is sensational eaten like this: the sweetness of the fruit and the salty *crème fraîche* tang of the cheese is memorable.

MAKING CHEESE AT HOME

To find out where to obtain starters and cheesemaking ingredients and equipment contact:

England
Specialist Cheesemakers Association, 17 Clerkenwell Green,
London ECIR ODP.
Tel: 020 7253 2114
e-mail: info@provtrade.co.uk
For starters: Ray Osbourne, tel: 01749 860666
For rennets: Christian Hansen, tel: 01488 689803

France
Fromage d'Outre-Manche (an association dedicated to bringing good British cheese to France), Château Nioton, Branne, France 33420.
Tel: 00 33 55 77 49 80
Fax: 00 33 57 74 99 76

Italy
Anfosc (an association pioneering traditionally made cheeses and those in danger of extinction), Viale Basento 108, 85100 Potenza.
Tel/fax: 00390 971 54661

USA
The American Cheese Society, 1523 Judah Street, San Francisco, California 94122.
Tel: 001 415 661 3844

Want to learn a bit more about cheesemaking? A basic cheesemaking course not only gives you an insight into the craft, but also outlines the various stages of manufacture, the different tastes of the milk from each type of animal as well as vegetal characteristics in grazing conditions. The courses last three days, from Tuesday to Thursday, and at the end you will get a certificate of attendance. If you don't live near the college, they have details of places to stay. The courses range from £150 to £300, but it is very hands-on and you will have the chance to actually make cheese from scratch.

Contact: Ms Chris Ashby, Milk Marque Product Development Centre,
Reaseheath, Nantwich, Cheshire CW5 6TA.
Tel: 01270 615502
Fax: 01270 611013
e-mail: chris.ashby@milkmarque.com

Try to obtain untreated muslin from a specialist cloth supplier such as Ian Mankin Ltd, 109 Regent's Park Road, London NW1 8UR – tel: 020 7722 0997, or 271 Wandsworth Bridge Road, SW6 2TX (mail order available) or from a good houseware/kitchen shop, or ask for Mull Muslin at the fabric department of John Lewis stores or Peter Jones in London.

All surfaces used for cheesemaking must be thoroughly cleaned and sterilized with a neutral cleaning agent. All pots and stainless-steel items must be sterilized for 5 minutes in boiling water and wooden spoons and cloths must be sterilized in boiling water for 20 minutes. Wash your hands thoroughly, with anti-bacterial hand-cleanser. Tie back your hair and make sure your clothing is protected with a large apron.

Home-made Fresh Cream Cheese

My mother told me how my grandmother used to make fresh cream cheese. Luckily for her the milk cart came past her house early each morning with fresh unpasteurized milk still warm from the cow. Grandma placed the jug on the floor of the kitchen beside the range, covered it with a cloth then left it overnight to allow the cream to separate from the milk. My mother's face lights up when she relates how the cream was skimmed off the top of the jug into a bowl then sprinkled with sugar for her to eat.

'It's a tasting pleasure I'll never forget.' Let's see if we can try to re-create something like it now.

- 1.5 litres of full-fat organic milk, as fresh as possible
- 3 tablespoons organic yoghurt
- a large piece of muslin, a tea-towel or a pillowcase, sterilized

Take a large ceramic or heavy pottery type jug, and sterilize it, as above. If the milk is cold, pour it into the jug and mix in the yoghurt. Put it into the oven at 150°C/300°F/Gas Mark 2 and leave it until the milk feels warm. Take it out and put the jug in a warm spot in the kitchen away from draughts or in an airing cupboard that's not too hot – that is, not in direct contact with a heater. You want a comfortable warmth, not a sweltering one. Cover the jug with a clean cloth and leave it.

After 48 hours the cream will have thickened and soured. Skim it off, leaving the watery solids in the jug. Place the cream in a dish, cover it with clingfilm, then put it into the fridge. Tip the contents of the jug into an ovenproof bowl or saucepan and either place it on top of the stove on a heat-diffusing mat at a low heat, or in the oven at 110°C/225°F/Gas Mark ¼. After 15–30 minutes the whey and curds will have separated. Place the muslin, pillowcase or tea-towel over a bowl and pour into the cloth the contents of the bowl or pan. Gather up the ends of the cloth and tie them with string. Hang the bag over a bowl and leave it to drip – lay a broom handle across two chairs and tie the bag to it to hang over the bowl. After 12 hours there should be no whey left in the bag, and the creamy cheese is now ready to eat. You could mix the whey into some cereal for your dog or cat, or if you have a pet pig even better: they hoover it up.

What to do with the cheese? You could mix it with the reserved soured cream, season it with a little fine salt and a tiny amount of sugar, put it back into the cloth and tie it up. Shape the bag into a rectangle or an oval and put a weight on top of it – for example, a board with a brick or a couple of cans: the liquid needs to be released but not entirely eliminated. Leave it for 1 hour then slide the cheese on to a plate and serve. Or serve the cheese straight from the bag into a bowl, with the soured cream in a separate bowl: spoon some cheese and cream on to your plate and add a little salt, a little sugar, some finely chopped herbs, onion and garlic, mix together and eat with fresh crusty bread. Alternatively, you could add the cheese and soured cream to berries or stewed fruits and sweeten it with sugar or honey (see Fruit Confit with Spiced Syrup, page 135). Try it served with Sweet and Sour or Soused Herrings (page 67), smoked salmon or salmon caviar.

Fresh Home-made Squacquerone Cheese

This fresh Italian cheese is an important element in traditional recipes, but with pasteurized milk it is difficult to achieve the required taste and texture. However, with a little ingenuity, and the best-quality cream, milk and yoghurt, you can reach a happy compromise. Similar Italian cheeses are Crescenza, very fresh Robiolina, or Robiola di Langhe, which is made with three types of milk.

To make around 450 ml
- 170 g best-quality cream cheese (from a good deli, not pre-packaged)
- 1 large tablespoon fresh cold *crème fraîche*
- 2 large tablespoons fresh cold buttermilk
- 3 large tablespoons untreated cold organic yoghurt
- juice of 1 lemon
- a little fine sea salt

Put the cream cheese into a bowl with the *crème fraîche* and blend them together. Stir in the buttermilk roughly, retaining the lumpiness of the cheese. Fold in the yoghurt and lemon juice, taste, and add salt if necessary. You want the mixture to have a little texture so be careful not to put too much pressure into the mixing. Cover the dish with clingfilm and refrigerate for at least 24 hours. The taste is creamy and fresh, and the flavours develop further the longer you keep it – up to 5 days.

Use this cheese in a pasta sauce, or mixed with spring onions and chopped ham piled on crisp salad leaves, or add honey and nuts to it as a dessert, or combine it with muesli for a healthy breakfast. I like it spooned over warm baby new potatoes with chives. Or try it with polenta and wild mushrooms. It also makes a lovely stuffing when mixed with shredded prosciutto and spooned into a chicken breast 'pocket'. Dip the chicken breast into beaten egg seasoned with salt and pepper, then coat it with a mixture of fine breadcrumbs, grated lemon rind and finely chopped thyme, and fry until it is golden brown on both sides.

Home-made Ricotta

This recipe is taken from Lynne Rossetto Kasper's *The Splendid Table*, an in-depth and lovingly written book of recipes from Emilia Romagna. This *ricotta* is especially creamy, and therefore perfect for using in cake recipes as well as savoury fillings. The finished cheese keeps for 4 days in the fridge.

Makes 450 g
- 3 litres organic whole milk
- 170 ml organic double cream
- 80 ml fresh lemon juice
- a pinch of fine sea salt (optional)

The cheese must be made in one session from start to finish – count on about 1½ hours, although much of this time is semi-unattended cooking. You should be in the kitchen, but you don't need to be hovering over the stove. The recipe may seem daunting in its detail, but it is really quite easy. Because cheesemaking is unfamiliar to many, the instructions lead you through the process step by step.

Heating the milk mixture slowly gives a soft ricotta curd time to develop. Fast heating hardens the curd, producing a very different cheese.

Stir together all the ingredients except the salt in a heavy saucepan with a non-reactive interior. Set the pan on a heat-diffusing pad over a medium-low heat. Cook for 40 minutes, or until the milk reaches 170°F on an instant-reading thermometer (the glass one for floating on liquids is best). Keep the heat at medium low. To keep the curd large, do not stir more than 3–4 times. If you lift it with the spatula, you will see sand-like particles of milk forming as the clear whey begins to separate from the curd. As the milk comes close to 170°F, the curds will be slightly larger, about the size of an uncooked lentil. When the temperature reaches 170°F turn the heat up to medium. Do not stir. Take 6–8 minutes to bring the mixture to 205°F at the centre of the pot. The liquid whey will be almost clear. By the time the cheese comes to 205°F the curd should mound on the spatula like a soft white custard. At this temperature the liquid will be on the verge of boiling, with the surface looking like mounds about to erupt. Turn off the heat and let the cheese stand for 10 minutes.

Line a colander with a double thickness of dampened muslin cheesecloth. Turn the mixture into it, and let it drain for 15 minutes or until the drained cheese is thick. Turn the cheese into a covered storage container, add the salt if you are using it, and refrigerate until needed. The whey can be used in Smoked Cheese and Corn Kernel Muffins (see page 145), or you can feed it to your cat or dog.

Fresh Cheese in Straw

The curd of a very fresh cheese is delicate to the touch, but quite sharp and strident in flavour. Its softness brings to mind a creamy dessert. If you are trying your hand at making fresh cheese, or can buy very fresh cream cheese, then why not have a go at preparing a dessert in the Poitou Charente-style? This is a region on the west coast of France famous for its Cognac and the delicious sweet wine Pineau des Charentes.

Place your freshly made cheese in the middle of a straw mat – confused already? Well, don't be! They aren't readily available I know but seek and ye shall find – or contact me! The practice of maturing and ripening cheeses on straw mats as we do in our cellars is in danger of being outlawed by the all-powerful bureaucracy in Brussels, and how long the two nice old ladies who make our mats for us in France are going to be able to carry on their business is anyone's guess. But if you feel as I do about respecting tradition and style when maturing cheese, then fight for the right to continue. However, if you can't get hold of a mat, wrap the cheese in sterilized double muslin.

Make sure the straw mat is clean and fresh, then place a quantity of fresh cheese in the centre – about 500 g – carefully roll it up, then secure the two ends with string, not too tightly, to hold the cheese intact. Immerse the cheese mat in brine, or the cheese's own whey, or make the 'bath' with plain bottled spring water. Leave the cheese overnight in its bath in a cool place, or at the bottom of the fridge.

To serve: take the mat or muslin out of the 'bath' and drain, then squeeze out any excess moisture. Open the mat and scoop the cheese into serving bowls. Drizzle over some very fresh single cream, if the taste of the cheese is too acid for your palate, sprinkle on some fine muscovado sugar, then douse it with a dessert wine such as the sweetly aromatic Pineau des Charentes. You will notice that the flavour of the cheese has a faint affinity with the straw mat. Do not re-use the mat.

Rogel with Dulce de Leche

This is a sweet, baked-milk cheese, rather like Gjetost, the dark, caramel-coloured, hard sweet cheese from Norway. However, in Europe and South America – where this recipe is famous – the baked milk is used as a spread, especially as a tea-time treat for children when bread is smeared with it then topped with slices of banana. The Dulce can be kept for at least a month in a clip-top preserving jar or jam jar with screw-top lid and stored in the fridge. For breakfast, try spreading some on toast or rolls, perhaps with a sprinkling of cinnamon. My dear friend Connie Aldao gave me this recipe and I like to serve it as a dessert with a Muscat or Moscato d'Asti wine. Connie works in Argentina with Francis Mallman, a superstar chef and restaurateur, well-known throughout the country. One of his restaurants is in Mendoza (1884 Restaurant Francis Mallman, Belgrano 1188, Godoy Cruz (5501), Mendoza; tel: 54-261 424 2698), the heart of the wine region, and he works closely with wine producers creating dishes to complement the delicious fruity rich ripe wines, which are a perfect accompaniment to spicy, full-flavoured sheep's milk cheese. Please note that the flour measurements are not exact: everything depends on the size and freshness of the eggs. *The quantity given is an estimate*, so sift it in spoon by spoon, until the required consistency is reached.

- 2 litres full-fat organic milk
- 1 kg caster sugar
- 1 teaspoon bicarbonate of soda
- 1 split vanilla pod

FOR THE ROGEL PASTRY

- 8 organic free-range large egg yolks (use the whites for meringues)
- 2 large organic eggs
- 240 g unsalted, light-textured butter (preferably from Charente), softened
- 250 ml dry white wine
- 500 g unbleached organic plain flour, sieved

To make the Dulce, take a large heavy-bottomed saucepan – use a heat-diffusing pad underneath it, if possible, so that the heat is evenly distributed. To avoid the mixture sticking to the bottom of the pan, insert a plate upside down on the base before pouring in the ingredients, or cover it with baking marbles – this also avoids the necessity to stir all the time. Put in all of the ingredients, bring to the boil, then reduce the heat and cook gently until a thick brown cream is formed. You will know that it is ready when you place a little blob on to a cool saucer and it sets quickly. Pour the Dulce into a sterilized earthenware pot or glass preserving jars, and allow it to cool before covering it with a waxed paper disc and popping on the lid.

To make the Rogel pastry, preheat the oven to 200°C/400°F/Gas Mark 6.

Beat the egg yolks, whole eggs and softened butter lightly until creamy, then stir in the wine. Beat in the flour – tablespoon by tablespoon – until you have a good firm pastry that's not too stiff and not too floppy; if you have made shortcrust pastry you will know the consistency required. Wet your fingers and divide the pastry into 10–12 balls. To roll them out, place a ball on a lightly floured surface, press it down to flatten it slightly and roll it into a thin disc. Place the discs on an oiled and lightly floured baking tray, prick them with a fork, and bake on the middle shelf until they are pale gold and crisp. Allow them to cool on a pastry rack. Sandwich them with the Dulce de Leche, dusting the top with icing sugar.

Fresh Cream Recipes

Whipped cream can be squeezed out of an aerosol, *crème fraîche* is seen in most supermarkets and thick *fromage blanc* or *frais* is available from most delicatessens. The difference between any of these and a home-made version is whether you want it ultra-fresh or with some sort of additive that will keep it fresher for longer. For sheer luxury and personal satisfaction the former comes up trumps. However, even a purist has to take a short-cut sometimes . . .

Fromage Blanc

You can use whole milk, semi-skimmed or skimmed, according to how rich you want the final result to be.

Makes 1.1 kg
- 2.3 litres whole or skimmed milk
- 1 packet direct-set *fromage blanc* starter or experiment with organic yoghurt with added active bacteria

In a sterilized heavy stainless-steel saucepan, heat the milk to 82°C/180°F. Then allow it to cool to 22°C/72°F – use a glass dairy thermometer, which floats on top of the milk to make it easier for you to see the temperature scale. Add the packet of *fromage blanc* starter to the milk and stir in. Cover the pan with a sterilized cloth then the saucepan lid and leave it to set at 22°C/72°F for 12 hours, or overnight perhaps, in the airing cupboard or in the oven at the lowest possible temperature with the door ajar. Line a colander with a layer of fine cheesecloth. Ladle the coagulated *fromage blanc* curd into it and allow it to drain for 6–12 hours or until the *fromage blanc* has reached the right consistency of creaminess. Make sure the temperature where the draining is taking place is at least 22°C/72°F.

Mascarpone

Most commercial mascarpone seems to be a *fromage blanc* with added cream, or *crème fraîche*, but the lightness of the cheese when it is home-made makes such a difference to, say, Tiramisu. Commercial mascarpone turns this dessert into a heavy, overpowering offering when it should be a light, fluffy cream with a rich, dark, coffee-liqueur-soaked biscuit.

Makes around 350–400 g
- 1.2 litres organic single cream, unpasteurized if possible
- ¼ teaspoon tartaric acid (from chemists) *or* 2 teaspoons liquid rennet

In a double boiler, heat the cream to 82°C/180°F. Add the tartaric acid or rennet and stir for several minutes. The cream should eventually thicken into a custard consistency with little bits of curd floating in it. If it doesn't, add a tiny bit more tartaric acid or rennet and stir for another 5 minutes. Be careful not to add too much as you don't want a grainy texture, or an overly bitter taste.

Line a stainless-steel colander with a double layer of sterilized fine cheesecloth. Pour the curd into the colander over the sink and leave it to drain for 1 hour. Then place the colander over a bowl, cover it with a clean cloth and allow it to drain in the fridge for 12 hours, or overnight. Pour the mascarpone into a food-storage container with a tight lid and keep it in the fridge. Use it within 10 days.

Fontainebleau

Served with fresh summer berries that have been quickly macerated in Maraschino liqueur with a little caster sugar, this creamy, fluffy white cloud is one of life's pure unadulterated pleasures to savour on a warm lazy day.

Enough for 4 good helpings
- 500 ml double cream
- 60 ml whole milk, as fresh as possible
- 1 scant tablespoon vanilla caster sugar

Pour the cream into a clean cold glass bowl, cover with clingfilm and leave for at least 3 days somewhere cool but not the fridge – a larder or a room without any central heating would do. It must look ripe but not have that cheesy taste. The milk should be added on the day you plan to eat it. Take the cover off the cream and sprinkle over the sugar. With a balloon whisk start to beat it and as it thickens and stiffens add the milk a little at a time until it becomes light as a feather. Spoon it gently into a serving bowl.

If you can trust your egg supplier – I know I can as I get mine from the Farmers' Market every week and they are not more than 2 days old – whisk 1 large or 2 medium egg whites until stiff and add to the creamy mass. You may want to shake a little more sugar over the top.

Crème Fraîche

Use your own home-made *crème fraîche* in the Borscht on page 85 – a divine taste of 'hot-pink' summer – and the Corn Chowder on page 87, with the first taste of early autumn's milky sweet corn-on-the-cob.

Makes 500 ml
- 500 ml double cream
- 2 tablespoons cultured buttermilk, made from a buttermilk starter, obtained from a cheesemaking supplier's or wholefood shops

Tip the cream into a very clean glass bowl and stir in the cultured buttermilk. Wrap the bowl in clingfilm and stand it in a warm airing-cupboard or draught-free kitchen overnight. By morning the mixture should have thickened. Put it into a serving pot or dish and cover tightly again with clingfilm, then refrigerate for several hours. Use within 2–3 days.

Crème Chantilly

This is a simple whipped and sweetened cream, with the addition of orange flower water. Serve it with the candied Fruit Confit (page 135) or Pain Perdu (page 136) for a match made in heaven. It goes without saying that it partners summer berries and is also rather good with Christmas pudding or mince pies. However easy the recipe seems, though, take great care with it.

Before you start, put the bowl and a large balloon whisk into the freezer for at least half an hour. The cold helps the cream expand and whip up lighter. Also, make sure that the cream and the milk are very fresh and very cold. To keep it so, try whisking the cream over a bowl filled with ice.

- 500 ml double cream
- 1–2 teaspoons vanilla icing sugar
- a few drops orange flower water or ½–1 teaspoon violet syrup (optional)
- 2 tablespoons full-fat organic milk or 1 tablespoon finely crushed ice (optional)

Tip the double cream into the bowl and start whipping with a balloon whisk, adding a teaspoon or two, according to your own taste, of icing sugar but the sugar should not dominate the cream. A few drops of orange flower water gives it a rather exotic taste, as does the violet-scented syrup, but if you use the latter, omit the icing sugar. To make the cream even more airy, whisk in the milk or the crushed ice.

BREAD AND SANDWICHES

Helen's Way (with Sandwiches)

My mother will be most embarrassed that I'm mentioning her in the cookery section of the book. She'd much rather I waxed lyrical about her innate dress sense and glamorous persona. She is Marlene Dietrich with attitude. But however much she loathes cooking, she has taught me one thing: how to make good sandwiches. Her criteria are easy and sensible.

First, use very good quality bread, which should be cut very thinly and the crusts removed. Butter it sparsely. Keep the fillings simple but of the best quality, always making sure the middle of the bread is nicely heaped, tapering down to the edges. Salad should not be too crisp and should be piled in the middle. The sandwich should always be cut into 4 pieces, and each piece should be enough for 2 bites. Her favourite fillings? Cream cheese and watercress; smoked salmon with thinly sliced deseeded cucumber and chopped hard-boiled egg, mixed with a little softened butter and fine sea salt, soft lettuce and mustard and cress. Simplicity in food, extravagance in personal appearance. Sadly, I am a disappointment to my mother!

Piadina Bread

This is a crisp flat bread in the style of, say, Calzone – perfect for scooping up soft creamy cheeses – and would benefit from being cooked on a flat griddle-type pan or a stone. However, since we're in modern times a little creative thinking will make things easier. If, like me, you go to art galleries and find yourself gazing dreamily at fine Italian canvases with their scenes of rich and plentiful feasting, you'll scrutinize the food to see what people ate hundreds of years ago. Most likely there, in a corner, will be some bread, which, most likely, is Piadina. I love old cookery books and discovering recipes like this to bring into use once more. There is, of course, a catch: some of the ingredients aren't very appropriate to our ideas on healthy eating, and in this recipe it's lard. Not just ordinary lard, though, a rendered-down *lardo*, which is a fragrant cured and spiced pork fat used rather like *pancetta*: sliced into thin ribbons and melted on *bruschetta* or used instead of oil in sauces and stews. Since the bread is light and yeast-free, I'm sure we can enjoy it without any fear – or if you feel guilty, go out and dig up the garden, or do fifty press-ups or take the dog for a brisk walk to compensate. You can make Piadina either by hand or in the food-processor, and I have given both methods below.

To render *lardo*: Pour enough water into a heavy saucepan barely to cover the bottom of the pan. Cut up the *lardo* (or, alternatively, ask the butcher for a little of the creamy fat that encases kidneys) and melt it very, very slowly so that the fat doesn't burn. Use it straight away or store it for a short period in the fridge, or freeze it if you prefer. Rendered *lardo*, either with butter or in place of it, makes a light, crisp, tasty pastry.

- 500 g unbleached stoneground organic plain white flour
- 1½ teaspoons fine sea salt
- ½ teaspoon baking powder
- 100 g rendered *lardo*, chilled, then crumbled
- 250 ml still spring water, lukewarm (use Italian if possible – I am quirky but, believe me, it makes a difference)

To make the dough by hand, stir together the dry ingredients in a large bowl or on a flat surface used for pastry-making, and rub in the *lardo* until the mixture looks like breadcrumbs. Pour in the water, mix it in and form the dough into a ball. Flour your hands and knead the dough on a lightly floured surface for 5 minutes or more until it becomes supple but not sticky. You can use it immediately, if you wish, or leave it covered with a cloth for 30–60 minutes at room temperature to relax. It is no sin to add a little more flour when kneading if you feel the dough is not 'coming together', but take care to keep it as supple as you can.

If you are using a food-processor, pour in the dry ingredients and pulse, then add the *lardo* and buzz again until the mixture looks like breadcrumbs. Pour in the water and pulse intermittently until you have a loose-textured mass. Take it out of the food-processor and drop it on to a lightly floured surface. Then, with your hands lightly floured, knead for 5 minutes or until the dough is supple but not sticky. Cover it with a clean kitchen towel and leave it to rest for 30–60 minutes, or you can use it immediately.

Divide the dough into 12 balls and roll them out into 18-cm rounds. Heat a griddle, if you have one, or a large heavy frying-pan that you know distributes heat evenly. To test whether the pan is hot enough put a few drops of water into it: if it evaporates in a couple of seconds it's ready. Brush or rub the pan with a little oil or lard, and cook the bread rounds one at a time. After about 30 seconds check the underside: if it is golden and mottled it is ready to turn (If you find that after 30 seconds the underside hasn't cooked sufficiently you may need to raise the heat.) Flip over and cook until it looks slightly drier and not as golden: the top side should look transparent and speckled. Pile the breads, interleaved with foil, and keep them warm in the oven, turned on low, as you cook the rest.

Serve warm, cut into 4, if you wish, brushed with olive oil and fresh rosemary, or sprinkled with oil and coarse sea salt. Piadina goes well with fresh Squacquerone (see page 28), accompanied by oven-roasted cherry tomatoes on the vine, or with any soft creamy cheeses. Or lightly brush a Piadina with olive oil, lay on it a slice of prosciutto, thinly sliced cooked ham or roasted chicken breast, with some thinly sliced mozzarella, or other soft fresh cheese – or, indeed, any cheese you like – and roll it up for an easy sandwich.

Variation: Cover half of the rolled dough circles with a soft cheese, such as mozzarella or fontina, and a little rich tomato sauce, fold over the other half to make a half-moon shape, seal the edges and place them on non-stick baking parchment on a baking sheet, then place them in the oven at 200°C/400°F/Gas Mark 6 for 5 minutes or so until they are golden.

Focaccia

If you are trying to sell your home, this is your secret weapon. The heavenly aroma of baking bread has contracts exchanged in no time. You don't need to be a master-baker to make Focaccia or wait hours for results.

- 30 g fresh yeast *or* dried (packet) yeast
- 800 ml still spring water, barely warm
- splash of olive oil
- 900 g strong plain white flour (Dove's Farm or Shipton Mill, if possible)
- 25 g sea salt
- fresh rosemary or thyme

In a large mixing bowl stir the yeast with the water until it has dissolved. Add the olive oil. Then gradually stir in the flour: mix each spoonful thoroughly into the liquid before adding the next. With the last scoop of flour add the salt.

Tip the dough out of the bowl on to a lightly floured table and start to knead. With the palm of your hand flatten the dough slightly to make an oval shape. Fold one end over the other to make a purse shape and with the heel of one hand push the dough away from your body to 'stretch' it again. Keep the other hand on the table to steady yourself and help you balance. Then fold the dough into the purse shape again, make a half turn and repeat. With practice you will build up a rhythm, knead and turn, knead and turn, until it is all worked thoroughly. Continue for 5–10 minutes until the dough is elastic and moist. You may want to sprinkle on a little more flour or a little water to attain the required consistency. Cover it with a clean tea-towel and leave it to rise in a warm, draught-free place for 45–60 minutes, no more than that.

Preheat the oven to 200°C/400°F/Gas Mark 6.

On a greased, lightly floured baking sheet, or a pizza stone if you have one, stretch the dough into a large rectangle about 40 cm × 25 cm – not too thin but not too thick. You may need 2 baking sheets. With a fork, or using your finger, stab indents into the Focaccia, then sprinkle over some roughly torn fresh rosemary or thyme. Leave it to rise again for another hour or so.

Before placing the Focaccia in the oven, sprinkle over some sea-salt crystals and drizzle olive oil into the indentations. Bake for 20–25 minutes until golden brown. You may like to add a savoury topping before you bake it: think along the lines of tomatoes, or slices of parboiled courgettes and aubergines, thinly sliced onions and, of course, cheeses – try crumbled fresh goat's cheese, mozzarella, or thick slices of young Taleggio with chunky cubes or slices of parboiled potato, thinly sliced onions and shreds of fresh sage, or with small cubes of soft fresh *pancetta*, or *lardons* with sliced onions.

My Night with Johnny Sandwich

It was going to be a close-run thing. I had to catch the last flight out of Paris to London and the evening was running forty minutes late, but Johnny Hallyday was crooning an Edith Piaf classic. Afterwards I ran for my life out of the venue to hail a taxi, passing the driver a 200-franc tip to get me to the airport in twenty minutes. My night with Johnny, as always, was exciting and dangerous. He has been – wrongly, *very* wrongly – compared to Cliff Richard. Excuse me, but I don't think our Cliff has had quite as many girlfriends and mistresses as my Johnny and his voice doesn't betray a lifetime of excess. I'd say Johnny sings something like Francis Rossi of Status Quo, but I think he would reckon he's more like Elvis Presley. But there's only one larger-than-life, rippling ready-for-action Johnny. Here's a juicy sandwich for the king of French rock – even though he's originally from Belgium.

- 1 fresh, crusty baguette
- unsalted butter
- 200 g Brie de Meaux cheese
- 1 Limburger or Maroilles cheese
- cornichons and caraway seeds
- salad

Limburger is a soft washed-rind cheese from Belgium, in the typically creamy yet powerfully strong style. The sticky red rind has a pungent aroma and you'll need a drink – I suggest beer, preferably an interesting Belgian one, which you will find in specialist beer shops.

Maroilles is from Thiérache in north-east France, and has the same characteristics as Limburger. There is a lovely apocryphal tale surrounding Maroilles and its related cheese Boulette d'Avesnes. Originally the cheese was made by monks, and during the turbulent Middle Ages, the abbey was ransacked and the fleeing friars grabbed what they could and raced for safety. Some took cheese to sustain them, but one was dropped in the herb garden. After a month the monks returned quietly to their abbey, and as they started to put everything back in order, the gardener found the cheese and took it into the kitchen. There it was tasted and found to be delicious. The monks then re-created the cheese by mashing the Maroilles and mixing it with a selection of herbs from the garden plus spices such as cloves, then remoulded it in the shape of a cone – Boulette d'Avesnes – and sometimes in other shapes like a dolphin, a compliment to the Dauphin, thus protecting themselves from further assaults.

Cut your baguette lengthways down the middle to make a long roll and spread it thinly with the butter. Slice the Brie over one half of the baguette then lay some salad on top. Slice the Limburger or Maroilles over the salad, followed by slices of cornichon. Scatter over some caraway seeds, then more salad. Pop the other half of the baguette on top and press it down gently, then cut it into 3 slanted portions.

Gunners Roll

I couldn't possibly run a business in Highbury without getting caught up with Arsenal fever. Also, with several French players on the team, I can discuss the matches with Eric our French cheese manager, without him getting bored – he comes from Toulouse so is more interested in rugby. Danny, my husband and business partner, and I try to go to home games, but when we can't plenty of customers come into the shop afterwards for post-match goodies and to go over the action with us. Here's a suitably Gallic sandwich to satisfy a hearty appetite.

- 1 large pitta bread
- 2 Toulouse sausages
- sunflower or peanut oil for frying
- 2–3 onions, sliced in thin rounds
- 3 medium potatoes, peeled, quartered and steamed until they are almost cooked
- salad
- Dijon or Grain mustard
- 200 g young Cantal cheese

Toast the pitta bread, then cut a deep pocket into it. Fry the Toulouse sausages in sunflower or groundnut oil until they are dark and crisp on the outside and clear juices run out when you prick them. Allow at least 8 minutes each side. Keep them warm while you fry the onions in oil until they are golden but not brown. Cut the potatoes into bite-sized chunks and when the onions are nearly done, add them to the pan and cook until they are nicely crisp – it shouldn't take too long. To assemble the sandwich, put some salad into the bottom of the pockets, then some sliced sausage with a little mustard, with onions and potatoes on top. Slice the Cantal and flash under the grill until the cheese starts to melt. Wrap the pitta in a paper napkin to prevent it collapsing. If you can't resist the temptation, pour over some HP sauce or tomato ketchup, and serve it with a six-pack. Singing and burping is an optional extra.

Cheese Sandwich

I'm always slightly amused by the amount of food people prepare to go on a picnic. I must admit, I used to prepare four-course feasts, much to the annoyance of my family – the number of boxes and pieces of kitchen paraphernalia loaded into the car caused many arguments. Then I got real. A sandwich in one pocket, a piece of fruit cake and an apple in another with a drink slipped into my bag and life was simple again. If I had time to watch a game of cricket these days, or gaze at the beautiful sunsets from Jocelyn's Beach in Chalkwell near Leigh-on-Sea, I would be more than happy to nibble away at my proper cheese sandwich.

- wholemeal or granary bread sliced from a whole loaf
- unsalted butter
- farmhouse Cheddar cheese, unpasteurized
- Tomato Chutney (see below)
- butterleaf salad and watercress
- sea salt

It's important that the bread is bought from a good bakery and is not pre-sliced – bread keeps fresher, anyway, if it is unsliced. Slice it to the thickness you prefer and spread it thinly with the butter. Slice the cheese with a sharp knife – don't grate it: you want to be able to experience the nutty, grainy texture mingled with the fruity flavour – and place it on the bread in a nice heap. Spread over the chutney and dress with the salad. Season with salt then put the other slice of bread on top. Gently press down, then cut it in half. Pack your sandwich in waxed paper before placing it in a paper sandwich bag.

Tomato Chutney

Makes 4 medium jars
- 2 red-skinned onions, finely sliced
- 2 tablespoons fruity but not too strong olive oil
- 2 cloves garlic, blanched then crushed to pulp
- 2 kg organic ripe tomatoes, or a mixture of green and red, peeled, seeded and finely chopped
- 200 g caster sugar
- 1 tablespoon freshly ground coriander
- ½ teaspoon hot paprika (Spanish for preference)

Sauté the onions in the olive oil until pale gold. Add the garlic, then the tomatoes, the caster sugar, coriander and paprika, and cook very gently for 1½ hours.

Let the chutney cool, then pour it into sterilized jars and put a circle of greaseproof paper on top. Seal with a lid. Keeps for up to 1 month.

Burratta with Prosciutto on Tapenade Bruschetta

Burratta is the softest creamiest curd, mostly sold in plastic, but we like to wrap it in green leek leaves. It looks almost like curdled mozzarella. It is so creamy and fragile that it must be eaten very fresh to enjoy the richness of the flavours before they sour. The prosciutto should be wafer-thin and hand-sliced: ours is a San Marcel ham from Aosta, fragrant from being cured in herbs and spices, and almost dissolves in the mouth. Don't use any old bread for the bruschetta, but slices from an open-textured Pagnotta weighing in at around 4 kg, made with *semola* (durum wheat) flour and baked in a wood-burning oven to a hard outer crust. Inside the bread is chewy, wonderful dipped into olive oil or, in this case, spread with an olive paste.

It might not be easy for you to buy a Pagnotta – dare I tell you that we import ours from Bari, in southern Italy, every week? However, a not too strong-tasting sourdough bread will be just as good, or the French *poilane* bread. As these breads are made in large sizes you will be able to buy a quarter of a loaf, or buy the whole thing and freeze whatever you don't use at once.

Cut the bread into serving slices around 2 cm thick. Toast or bake them in the oven at 180°C/350°F/Gas Mark 4 until pale golden but not too highly baked. Spread on top of the warm bread a slick of black olive paste. You can buy it in your local deli or make it yourself by mincing stoned black or green olives and mixing them with a fruity olive oil until you have a thick paste (don't buy ready-stoned olives as the taste will be less pronounced). For each slice of bread you will need 50 g of olives (either Provençal black or green ones, or the tiny Ligurian Taggiasche ones). Stone the olives and lay them on the olive paste, then cover with some ham and 2 slices of Burratta (each around 1 cm thick). Place the bread on a lightly oiled baking sheet and return it to the oven for about 5 minutes or until the cheese has started to melt and spread.

A Sort of Welsh Rarebit

Rinse a couple of salted anchovies until all the salt has been removed, pat dry on paper towel, then carefully remove all the flesh, making sure none of the bones remain. Blend the fish with unsalted butter until it is quite smooth – the amount of butter you use depends on how fishy you like it. Slice thinly and toast a piece of *poilane* sourdough bread, or a similar English-style sourdough or *pain de campagne*, then spread thickly with the anchovy butter. Pile thin slices of a medium-matured Gorwydd Caerphilly or Appleby's Cheshire, or a crumbly, tangy cheese of your choice, and heap it into a dome. Shake over a few drops of Worcestershire or another fruity brown sauce and grill until the cheese has melted and turned golden.

Dipped Croque Monsieur

Take some slices of white bread, butter them, then lay on some Gruyère or Emmental-style cheese and add a sparse sprinkling of sea-salt crystals. Sandwich them together, pressing down to seal, then dip them into beaten egg followed by medium matzo meal or fine breadcrumbs. Place them on an oiled baking-sheet and grill them until they are golden on both sides.

Bruschetta with Gorgonzola Dolce Cremificato, Walnuts and Mantovana Melon

One of my rather cynical theories is that bruschetta became popular with restaurateurs and caterers because it's a fancy name for stale bread! But I'm all for it – I hate to waste good bread just because it's a day or two old.

Take a slice of crusty farmhouse-style, rather open-textured bread and brush it over with a fruity olive oil. Thinly slice a creamy Gorgonzola *dolce* and pile it generously on to the bread. Toast some walnuts a little and scatter them on, crushing them as you go. On top lay slices of ripe Mantovana, or another orange-fleshed melon with a sweet taste and aroma.

Serve with a chilled Moscato d'Asti semi-sweet wine from the Piedmont area.

Croque Style Curnonsky

Monsieur Curnonsky was aptly named the Prince of Gastronomy in France and reigned supreme until his death at the age of eighty-four in 1956. 'Cooking, that's when things taste like what they are,' he said, meaning that it is only when you cook from scratch, rather than buying ready-made meals, that curiosity leads you to combine ingredients and discover flavours you wouldn't have been aware of if you were just reheating something. He was revered and feared by chefs and restaurateurs in France, not because of his acid pen but for his knowledge and sense of good taste.

He treated food styles like political parties: far right was precise and traditional *haute cuisine*; far left was experimental. (It would be interesting to think up dishes to represent today's politicians – amusing and enlightening at the same time!) Restaurant and food writers today should study his work and follow Curnonsky's lead: he understood every facet of the food industry and how a meal or dish should be prepared course by course. He showed no favouritism and was dismissive of chefs who no longer felt the need to be in front of the range once they had achieved Michelin status. He always had a comment on the cheeseboard offered, unlike many restaurant reviewers of today.

- 100 g Roquefort cheese, preferably Carles for strength
- 50 g unsalted Charente butter, at room temperature, plus a little extra
- 2 slices medium-sliced white bread, with or without crusts
- 1 large slice farmhouse-style ham

Gently mash the Roquefort so that it does not lose its slightly gritty texture, and mix it with the softened butter. Spread it on the bread. Place the ham on one slice and sandwich together with the other. In a frying-pan melt some butter until it foams and fry the sandwich on both sides until it is golden brown. Lift it out carefully and drain it on paper towel. Serve with a green salad dressed with walnut oil and crumbled toasted walnuts.

Camembert Toasts

For each slice of bread – *pain de campagne* or a light sourdough or *pain de poilane* – roast around 50 g walnuts in a preheated oven at 200°C/400°F/ Gas Mark 6 for 5 minutes or until they are just starting to become golden. Grate them finely and set them aside. Toast the bread on one side only, and spread the Camembert (rind removed), creamed with a little *fromage blanc* to a rich, smooth paste, on the untoasted side. One Camembert will coat 2 decent slices of bread. Cover the cheese-topped bread with the walnuts, then cut it into triangles or rectangles or neat bite-sized pieces. Place them on a non-stick baking sheet and bake for 5 minutes or until the walnut topping is nicely toasted. Serve as an appetizer.

And Some Final Ideas

Try dark rye bread with pecan nuts and chunky slices of Gruyère or Beaufort or some other fruity, grainy-textured cheese. Mix some wholegrain mustard with a little fruity white wine into some softened unsalted butter and spread this on the bread before you lay the cheese on top. Eat either toasted or untoasted. See also Smoked Salmon and Cream Cheese Bagel, page 49.

A Travelling Tale

MANHATTAN, NEW YORK

*I*t may only be eighteen miles long, but Manhattan Island is packed with every nationality and divided up into sectors where you can flirt with sights, sounds and aromas as you explore. Whether you are in Chinatown, or Little Italy, Greenwich Village, Clinton, Alphabet City, East Village, NoLita, TriBeCa, SoHo or – if you dare venture way uptown along Atlantic Avenue – the newly gentrified Harlem or the Bronx across the East river, you will be amazed and delighted at your discoveries and the variety of shops – New Yorkers love to shop and they love to eat. However, my favourite part of New York is Brooklyn, which has spread its well-muscled arms and embraced me. What grabs the eye first are the wide-open spaces, the red-brick houses, and great little shopping areas not too far from Brooklyn Bridge. Catch a city sunset as you walk over the bridge back to Manhattan on a Sunday and you are reliving your favourite Woody Allen movie, or humming a Gershwin melody. Buy a bagel with lox and cream cheese, or better still make one yourself.

Split the bagel in half and scoop out the doughy bread inside to make a channel, then spread a thick layer of good-quality cream cheese in the shells. Sprinkle over a few grains of coarse sea salt and finely chopped dill or fennel fronds. Generously layer over slices of smoked salmon – the sweeter London smoke variety is not too salty or smoky – then squeeze on lemon juice and sprinkle over some cayenne rather than black pepper to pep-up the taste. Don't throw away the scooped-out bread: you can dry it out in the oven then crush it into fine crumbs, which you can store in an airtight container or freeze, or you may prefer to keep them in a plain paper bag sealed with a tag.

You wouldn't believe America has fine cheeses – when a burger contains a slice of processed yuck, a product exists called 'Cheese Strings' and you can buy cans of Spray Cheese. All delightful I'm sure, but I'll pass on the taste test. I was amazed to find some of the best-tasting cheeses in a small cheese shop called Murray's on Bleecker Street in Greenwich Village. It looks like a European cheese shop, with part of the counter open rather than all behind glass, and the aromas of the farmhouse and farmyard pervade the shop. The helpful, knowledgeable staff make the visit all the more enjoyable. I was given slivers of cheese to taste and each was a revelation. Sally Jackson cheeses, from Oroville deep in the Okanogan Highlands, not far from the Canadian border in Washington State, are true individuals. The one I liked best was wrapped in chestnut leaves, a semi-hard sheep's milk cheese tasting fruity with a sweet sharpness that reminded me of Spanish cheeses. Another sheep's milk cheese that always wins prizes is Vermont Shepherd from the Major farm in Putney, Vermont. You could almost be fooled into believing it was from the Pyrenees, as the taste and texture have all the intrinsic qualities of an Ossau cheese – fruity, nutty, with a rugged bite. The Cypress Grove goat's cheeses, made in McKinleyville, California, with imaginative names such as Bermuda Triangle, Pee Wee Pyramid, Sempervirens and my favourite Humboldt Fog, have that clean nutty tang that comes with using high-quality fresh milk and maintaining exemplary cheesemaking standards. The Humboldt Fog is coated in charcoal ash with white bloomy moulds as a veil, and inside the cheese has a thin layer of ash rippling through the centre.

For sheer versatility as a culinary and cheeseboard choice, Maytag Blue, from the Stevens' farm in Newton, Iowa, is hard to beat. Made from unpasteurized milk, the cheese is similar in style to a French Bleu des Causses – rich, buttery and fruity-tasting – making it suitable for cooking as well as a table cheese. And there are the aged Monterey Jack, or Gouda-style cheeses, tiny fresh Coach button cheeses, or the aged Cheddar-style Shelburne. In Manhattan, Picholine, on West 64th

Street, a Michelin-starred restaurant, offers a display of artisan cheeses to match even France. The owner-chef, Terrence Brennan, visited us to see how we run our shop and cellars. His love of farmhouse cheeses has prompted him to open his own specialist cheese shop, called Artisan – situated on Park Avenue (midtown) – and a bistro serving original cheese dishes – with maturing rooms to keep the cheeses in good condition. It is a courageous venture, given the intense opposition by the draconian U.S. Food and Drug Administration, which exists to standardize food production and animal-rearing methods, and reins in enterprises such as artisan cheese-makers.

With this in mind I'm hoping to persuade Danny to take me skiing in Colorado instead of his favourite Trois Vallées in France, not because I want a change of scene but to find out more about a new blue cheese from Kristi and Tom Johnson called Bingham Hill Rustic Blue. They only started selling their cheese at the end of 1999, and it has been compared to a British-style robust Stilton. I'll have to think of something interesting to get him to Fort Collins – hopefully it's not too far away from the ski slopes – as I am curious to meet new cheesemakers working on such a small scale.

Not far from Bleecker Street is the arty SoHo area where ultra-fashionable shops sit side by side with idiosyncratic galleries, bars, cafés, restaurants and knick-knack stalls. If you fancy looking at a room full of earth – for that is all there is to view, and it has been there since 1977, regularly watered and hoed – then I recommend Earthworks on Greene Street, or the Gagosian Downtown Gallery on Wooster Street (less intimidating than the uptown penthouse gallery). However, a must-see is Joe's Dairy on Sullivan Street, which makes fresh mozzarella in the back kitchen – from the shop you can glimpse the huge pans of bubbling water with the mozzarella bobbing about on top. Cross Broadway to Little Italy and you'll find Alleva Dairy on Delancey Street, the oldest cheese shop in America – so I'm told – and you'll have no difficulty in believing you're in a back-street shop in Rome when you buy some fresh home-made ricotta for your pasta that evening. Not far away is Eileen's famous cheesecake shop at 17 Cleveland Place, between Kenmare and Spring Streets, where I tasted a jaw-jamming cake that was simply wonderful. Don't be tempted by the various flavours and additions: go for the original plain version – it's the best.

If you have time for lunch, go to 25 Cleveland Place, where the delightful Le Jardin bistro, with its lovingly tended outside vine-covered courtyard, is a quiet gustatory oasis in this bustling city. Then venture into the East Village area of Elizabeth Street and Mott Street, where many new young dress and craft designers show their wares. In Elizabeth Street a dinky butcher specializes in veal – the happily reared kind. It isn't really a shop, more a weathered, homely Neapolitan back kitchen, where an elderly gentleman slices his exquisite meat with such precision that you don't need to pound the slices to get them into even rounds. All they need is a dusting of flour before you pan-fry them in olive oil and butter then top them with slices of oozing fresh mozzarella, Burratta or Crescenza, then flash them under the grill to 'relax' the cheese. A little salse of basil, olive oil, capers and lemon zest, crushed in a pestle or blender and drizzled over the top, finishes them off nicely. You could use chicken escalopes instead, but I believe the flavour and texture of veal is perfect.

Round the corner in Mott Street, between Houston and Prince Streets, is my favourite place to ease aching feet: Café Gitane. The blue jackets of the waiting staff remind me of the farmer's jackets we wear in La Fromagerie, and the café attracts a hip, cool clientele. The sombre red brick of St Patrick's Church is opposite, and gives the street a cloister-like atmosphere.

My visits to New York would not be complete without a wander round the Farmers' Market on Union Square: I love chatting to the stallholders and finding my favourite pretzels – crisp and warm – my favourite carrot cake, my favourite poppyseed biscuits, my favourite salad mix – and what about a lump of wheat grass to whiz up in a juicer for a quick energy fix? Then there are my favourite little fresh goat's cheeses, and my favourite cup of warmed spiced apple juice . . . It never ends.

There are the cocktails too. I think some of the best and strongest drinks I have ever had were in New York – although my memory is a little fuzzy. Whether it's a Cranberry Vodka Cocktail or a Chocolate

Martini, the best time to start drinking is four p.m., as far as I am concerned, then the rest of the evening flows along beautifully. When I get home I try to re-create my cocktail moments, but it was only when I brought a violet liqueur back from Toulouse that I concocted, with the help of my treasured old recipe book *The Vicomte in the Kitchen* (*circa* 1934), an aromatic, floral, creamy martini to set my brain fizzing again.

Cocktails such as dry and sweet martinis, the Manhattan, and all others not made with egg, milk or syrups should not be shaken, but as I like to add some really fresh thick *crème fraîche* to mine, I invested in a cocktail shaker to produce the required consistency and chill.

Violet Chocolate Cream Cocktail

Fill your shaker half full of ice and pour in 50 ml Violette liqueur, 30 ml vodka, 20 ml clear chocolate liqueur, 1 tablespoon fresh thick *crème fraîche*. Pop on the lid and shake. Strain into a cold martini glass and sprinkle over crystallized violet petals. It doesn't taste strong, but after two of these you'll start feeling decidedly mellow.

LUNCHES, SUPPERS AND SAVOURIES

Braised Balsamic Onions with Grilled Goat's Cheese

Bittersweet flavours accent foods like cheese, salad leaves and meats, such as duck, or chunky fish like cod.

For 4 people, cut 3 red-skinned onions into chunky pieces and pack them into an ovenproof dish. Douse them evenly with a good olive oil, scatter over some torn sage leaves and a little coarse sea salt, and bake at 180°C/350°F/Gas Mark 4 until the onions are caramelized. Take out the dish and drain off the oil (which you can use to sauté some potatoes perhaps). Place the onions in a hot frying-pan, pour over a wine-glass of red wine and cook rapidly to reduce. Lower the heat then add a tablespoon or two of the best balsamic vinegar you can afford and continue to cook until the onions taste richly sweet and sour and are almost jammy. Thinly slice 2 Crottins de Chavignol, or a similar semi-dry goat's cheese, over the onions, sprinkle with roughly crushed black peppercorns then place the pan under the grill until the cheese begins to melt and toast to a lovely golden colour. Serve on a toasted brioche, or slices of sourdough bread.

A side salad of rocket and bitter salad leaves, dressed in a peppery olive oil, would add an extra piquancy. Or you could serve the onions as a cold accompaniment to Raclette (see page 81) or Fondue (page 77), or with a chunky slab of pan fried cod: leave its skin intact and grate over the flesh a dry goat's cheese; then add a smattering of chopped fresh thyme and black peppercorns before flashing it under the grill to 'relax' the cheese rather than melt it. Sit the fish on the braised onions and partner it with a side dish of fragrant potatoes, which you have parboiled and skinned then dried in a saucepan over a low heat. Sauté them in olive oil and butter with garlic shards, rosemary sprigs and coarse sea salt until they are golden and crusty around the edges.

Goat's Cheese and Walnut Pâté with Walnut Oil Watercress Dressing

In early September we see the arrival of wet or 'green' walnuts in their grubby, unwashed shells. The walnut skins are easy to peel off and the white nut has that fresh crunch and milky sweetness that works beautifully with the rich autumn goat's milk cheeses.

Serves 4

FOR THE PÂTÉ

- 400 g soft fresh goat's cheese, rind removed
- 200 g wet walnuts, skinned, lightly toasted then loosely crushed
- 2 tablespoons finely chopped celery leaves
- 1 tablespoon finely chopped chervil
- 1 teaspoon finely grated lemon peel, plunged into boiling water for a minute, drained, refreshed in cold water and patted dry on paper towel
- juice of ½ lemon

FOR THE DRESSING

- 6 tablespoons walnut oil
- 1 bunch watercress, picked over, thick stems removed then liquidized
- 2 sprigs rosemary
- lemon peel, treated as above
- 1 fresh bay leaf, roughly torn
- ½ vanilla pod
- fine organic sea salt, and freshly ground black pepper

- finely chopped celery, shredded chicory, watercress and other interesting salad leaves

Blend together all the pâté ingredients, form the mixture into a swiss roll shape, and wrap it in clingfilm. Chill it until it is firm, then cut into portions.

To make the dressing, stir all the ingredients together in a bowl, scraping the seeds from the vanilla pod and mixing them in, then cover it with clingfilm. Let the dressing marinate for an hour or two for the flavours to develop.

To serve, place a heap of salad leaves in the centre of a plate and drizzle over a little of the strained dressing. Place pâté on top, and drip some more strained dressing around the edges of the plate in random artistic blobs. A slice of bruschetta, made with *pain de campagne* or sourdough bread brushed with rosemary-flavoured oil then toasted, goes well with this.

Provençal 'Trouchia'

This is a sort of omelette, which makes a great picnic or lunch dish because it's just as good warm or cold. The taste of Trouchia is pure summer, when young, tender leafy vegetables bring a delicate piquancy to it.

- around 1 kg leafy Swiss chard or spinach, tough stalks removed, washed, dried and shredded
- 1 large bunch chervil, tough stalks removed
- 1 small bunch flat parsley, tough stalks removed
- 8 large free-range organic eggs
- 200 g finely grated young – 26-month – Parmigiano Reggiano, or Grana, or a hard, grainy, fruity cheese
- sea salt and freshly ground black pepper
- 4–6 tablespoons good-flavoured olive oil

Preheat the oven to 180°C/350°F/Gas Mark 4.

Mix the shredded chard or spinach with the chervil and parsley. Break the eggs into a bowl and beat gently. Fold in the cheese, then the leaves and herbs. Season judiciously with salt and grind over some black pepper.

In an ovenproof omelette pan heat half of the olive oil until it is hot but not smoking. Pour in the egg mixture and stir until it starts to fluff up and bubble. Cover with a lid and put the pan into the oven for around 15 minutes, until the underside of the omelette is golden brown. Remove it from the oven and slide it upside down on to a plate. Wipe the omelette pan with a paper towel then put it back on to the stove, pour in the rest of the oil and heat it, then put the omelette back into the pan, the uncooked side on the bottom. Put the lid back on and replace it in the oven for a further 15 minutes, until the underside is golden brown.

Remove it from the oven and slip the omelette on to a plate. Allow it to cool a little before cutting it into portions. Serve either warm or cold.

Cooked Ham with Fried Eggs and Melted Manchego on Toast

I like my fried eggs to have crisp lacy edges, the yolk not too runny but not too cooked either. I never order fried eggs in restaurants or hotels because they are taught not to cook them like that – it's dead common apparently. More fool them, I say. This is my favourite late breakfast or early supper treat.

Take some thick slices of white bread, toast them and smear them lightly with unsalted butter. Fry hand-sliced cooked ham in a little butter – I like mine not overcooked. Lay it on the toast. Wipe out the frying-pan then heat it until it is hot and pour in either oil, butter or your preferred frying agent. Heat it until it is hot but not smoking, crack in the eggs – one large organic egg per slice of bread – and fry until the whites have that crisp lacy edge and the yolk is still soft. Place the eggs on top of the ham, then shave over some Manchego sheep's milk cheese, or Pecorino, or a similar hard cheese – use a potato-peeler to achieve very thin ribbons.

Sautéed Calves' Liver with Mozzarella di Bufala

The combination of offal with the light, somehow mossy flavour of mozzarella is delicious. I first encountered this pairing at my favourite local restaurant where Eric Guignard is the chef. As he's from Provence, he had no hang-ups about using ingredients from around the Mediterranean, dipping into Italy or Spain for inspiration. His signature dish was *foie gras* with a slice of buffalo mozzarella resting on top and melding into it – a stylish dish, and, with a glass of spicy almost liquorice-tasting Alsace Gewürztraminer, it made an impressive starter. The recipe I have concocted here is a main course, which should be served with simple green vegetables, such as steamed spinach or fine green beans, or salad.

Calves' liver bought ready-packed is usually too thinly sliced for this dish, so I suggest you get it from a butcher.

Serves 2 as a main course, 4 as a starter
- 500 g sliced calves' liver, around 2.5 cm thick, with any white membrane cut away
- plain flour, mixed with a grinding of black pepper, to coat the liver
- 3–4 tablespoons Puglian, or Ligurian, olive oil
- 100 g *pancetta*, chopped into small cubes
- 2 tablespoons balsamic vinegar
- 250 g chanterelles, smallest you can buy (optional)
- 1 glass dry, fruity white wine
- 300 g freshest possible buffalo mozzarella
- basil leaves

Cut the liver into chunky pieces and coat them in the seasoned flour, shaking off any surplus. In a heavy frying-pan heat the oil, enough to coat the base of the pan. Pan-fry the cubes of *pancetta* until they are just translucent, then pop in the liver and continue to cook until it is brown on both sides – around 7 minutes on each side. Put in the balsamic vinegar and stir to coat the liver in it. Throw in the chanterelles then pour over the wine, let it bubble, turn down the heat and simmer for around 5 minutes. Test the liver for required 'doneness' – skewer a piece, and if it is too rare cook it a little longer. Have the mozzarella at room temperature and slice it thinly. Put the liver on the plates, lay slices of cheese on top, then toss over some roughly shredded basil leaves and serve at once. If you've forgotten to bring the cheese to room temperature, slice it over the liver and flash it under a medium hot grill for 30 seconds to 'relax' it.

Note: Use a good balsamic that is at least six years old if you can – the flavour is much improved.

Hamburger with Gruyère Cheese and Fried Onions

Ask your butcher to mince your meat freshly, but don't turn up at their busiest time! A properly made hamburger with a gooey cheese topping and fried onions is a million miles away from McDonald's. If you use clarified butter to fry the onions they will be sweet and crisp, but Mazchik vegetable fat, available from kosher delis, which is like pure rendered chicken fat (an ultra-sensational agent for frying onions – only the thought of terminal heart failure prevents me using it often), is healthier.

Makes 2 hamburgers
- 200 g lean sirloin steak, minced finely
- 115 g lean chuck steak, minced finely
- ½ large carrot, peeled and grated
- 1 onion, peeled and grated
- fine sea salt and freshly ground black pepper
- 1 teaspoon chopped thyme
- 1 egg, beaten lightly
- 1 tablespoon sunflower oil, for frying

FOR THE FRIED ONIONS
- 2 large firm-textured onions suitable for frying
- 4 tablespoons clarified butter, vegetable fat or sunflower oil
- mushroom ketchup
- Worcestershire sauce
- a little red wine or water

FOR THE CHEESE TOPPING
- 2 chunky slices Gruyère, Comté, Beaufort, or similar fruity-tasting smooth-textured cheese such as Fontina, Gabriel, Appenzeller, Mahon or even Cheddar
- wholegrain mustard

Place the two meats in a bowl and mix them together with dampened hands. Add the carrot and onion and mix well. Don't work the meat too hard but use loose relaxed hand movements. Add a good pinch of salt, season well with black pepper, and mix in the chopped thyme. Bind together with the egg. Form into 2 large patties or 4 small ones.

Chop the onions in half and slice them into fine strips. Heat the fat or oil in a heavy frying-pan until it is hot but not smoking, and sauté the onions until they are golden brown. Keep them warm in an ovenproof dish in the oven at 150°C/300°F/Gas Mark 2.

Put the hamburgers into the same pan with a tablespoon of oil, and fry them for 4 minutes on each side if you want them rare – press the top of the meat to check: if it feels soft and squashy it is ready – or continue cooking for another 3 minutes if you want them medium, when they will offer a little more resistance to being pressed. If you want them well done they will feel firmer. Remove them from the pan and keep them warm on a heated serving dish.

Now scrape up all the lovely fried bits and pieces in the pan. Pour out most of the oil and shake in some mushroom ketchup and Worcestershire sauce with the wine or water, scraping up the bits until you have a little syrupy sauce – tip in any juices that might have escaped from the hamburgers while they were resting on the plate.

Turn the grill on high. Lay the slices of cheese, one side spread with the mustard, on the hamburgers, mustard side on the meat, and flash under the grill until the cheese starts to melt.

Heap a portion of fried onions on each plate, place the cheese-topped hamburger either on top or to the side, drizzle a little of the sauce around the edges and serve with creamed potatoes and salad. Or, if you must, sandwich the onions and the hamburger with the glaze dribbled over the top in a toasted sesame bun.

Pork Chops with Cheese Topping and Grated Potato Galette

With all the food scares and concern about how animals are reared and moved across Europe, it becomes clearer and clearer to me that specialist breeders, or butchers who belong to the Q Guild, are the best bet to safeguard our health and maintain the traditional methods of farming by individuals rather than large, anonymous businesses. A few farms use organic methods and rely on biodynamic feeds and homeopathic medication. Long-established pig breeds, such as Gloucester Old Spot and Tamworth, with a succulent rim of fat and the meat tasting of the apples and acorns that the pigs eat, should not be the stuff of fairy stories evolving into a hazy memory of times past. Get in touch with Heritage Prime in Dorset (01297 489304), Pedigree Meats of Herefordshire (01600 890296), and Northfield Farm in Rutland (01664 474271), and for Aberdeen Angus beef contact Donald Russell Direct (01467 629660).

Serves 4
- 6 large potatoes suitable for frying, e.g. Charlottes or King Edwards, peeled, chopped and roughly grated
- sea salt and freshly ground black pepper
- 1 small clove garlic, peeled and finely chopped
- 1 tablespoon sunflower oil
- 50 g unsalted butter
- 4 large pork chops
- good-quality olive oil
- 4 tablespoons grated cheese, such as Beaufort, Comté, San Andrea, Montasio, or similar Gruyère-style cheese
- 1 tablespoon Dijon mustard
- 1 tablespoon *crème fraîche*

Peel, wash and grate the potatoes (use the larger holes on a hand grater) into a large bowl. Add salt and pepper, a couple of good pinches, and the finely chopped or grated garlic and mix well. In a large heavy non-stick frying-pan, preferably with a lid, heat the sunflower oil and drop in the potato mixture. When you have turned it thoroughly in the hot oil, dot over small nuggets of unsalted butter and press down until you have formed the potatoes into a thick galette. Half cover the pan with the lid and cook over a medium heat for 30 minutes. Turn the galette half-way through to brown the other side.

Rub the chops well with the olive oil and grill or pan-fry them for

5–10 minutes, according to their thickness, or use one of those heavy cast-iron ribbed griddles. (Oil the meat rather than the pan or the kitchen will fill with smoke.) Mix together the cheese, mustard and *crème fraîche*, and smooth evenly over the chops. Place them under a hot grill until the cheese mixture is golden and bubbling. Take out the chops and put them on a warmed serving plate to rest for 5 minutes, covered loosely with foil.

Cut the potato galette into 4 portions. Put a piece beside each chop. Serve with a green salad dressed simply with good olive oil and a splash of balsamic vinegar, drizzled with any juices released from the meat while it was resting.

Note: If you don't want to use French or Italian cheeses, try instead a semi-matured St Cuthbert's Cave from Wooler, Northumbria, a medium-matured Coolea from Co. Cork, or a Caerphilly or Cornish Yarg if you prefer a milder cheese.

Spicy Chorizo Sausages with Manchego

I love chorizo sausages cooked until their caramelized crusty skins smoulder. When your teeth bite through the skin a whole new set of expressions appear on your face as the heat and flavours of the spicy meat engulf your senses. Eat really spicy sausages while they are still very hot from the pan to get the full impact. With fingers of aged Spanish sheep's milk Manchego from La Mancha, you have a perfect partnering of full-bodied tastes. As an appetizer it's hard to beat.

I've just had another thought: mash up some very fresh goat's cheese, or goat's curd, or the Piedmontese ricotta called Sairass – it's a cow and sheep's milk soft, billowy cheese that's just a few days old – and pile it into a dish. Add a little lemon juice or grated lemon zest to give it an added acidity. Then dip your very hot spicy sausages into the very cold creamy cheese for an interesting mixture of hot zappy meat and cool, tangy cream cheese.

Involtini

Stuffed and rolled meat or fish is typical of southern Italian cooking, especially when the rolls are cooked in a rich tomato sauce. These rolls include Pecorino cheese: try the Tuscan semi-matured black-rinded one, or even the Pienza Marzolina, which is softer, more pliable, and melts easily, or perhaps Crescenza from Piedmont, fresh, creamy but supple-textured. When tomatoes are in season, you might prefer to substitute fresh roasted ones for the canned ones in the recipe: take 1.5 kg vine tomatoes and roast them on the bottom shelf of the oven at the lowest setting with olive oil and herbs for at least 3 hours or preferably overnight. Take off the skins before you use them.

Serves 4
- 4 veal escalopes
- approximately 16 thin slices Pecorino cheese
- approximately 24 not-too-thin slices fresh soft salami
- thyme or sage, finely chopped
- seasoned flour, for coating the escalopes
- oil and butter, for frying
- good-quality extra-virgin Tuscan olive oil, to serve

FOR THE TOMATO SAUCE
- at least 120 g unsalted butter
- 2 medium-large red onions, peeled and finely chopped
- 2 large carrots, peeled and diced
- 1 heaped tablespoon tomato purée or Italian Tomato Concentrate (in cake form)
- 2 × 500 g cans plum tomatoes
- 1 teaspoon caster sugar
- freshly ground black pepper
- fresh thyme or flat-leaf parsley, chopped
- sea salt (optional)

First, make the tomato sauce. In a heavy-bottomed pan, melt the butter until it is foaming and sauté the onions and carrots. When they are golden, but not caramelized, add the tomato purée or concentrate, and stir or let it melt into the vegetables. Put in the tomatoes and mash them roughly. Add the sugar, a grinding of black pepper and the thyme or parsley. Taste the sauce before you add salt – if you are using the tomato concentrate, you may find that the sauce doesn't need it. Cover the pan and leave the sauce to cook very slowly until it is very thick. This will take up to 1 hour.

Now for the veal. Preheat the oven to 180°C/350°F/Gas Mark 4. Take the escalopes and bash them flat with a rolling pin. Lay over them thin slices of Pecorino, then the salami. Scatter over the thyme or sage. Roll up the escalopes and secure them with thread tied round them in 3 places, or with cocktail sticks. Dust the rolls with flour. Heat the olive oil and butter in a frying pan until the butter is foaming and fry the rolls for a few minutes until they are nicely coloured, but not cooked through. Lift them out with a slotted spoon and place them in a casserole. Pour around them the tomato sauce – it should not entirely cover them so use, say, around 2 tablespoons per roll. (Keep any leftover tomato sauce in the fridge or freezer – it is tremendously versatile and you are sure to find a use for it!) Bake for around 20 minutes. To serve, drizzle over a little of the Tuscan extra-virgin olive oil.

Note: The tomato sauce can be served alongside baked goat's cheese – or, in summer, combine it with fresh pasta ribbons and top with ultra-fresh crumbled ricotta (either cow's milk or sheep or goat's milk – but it must be very fresh). Try it with mascarpone too. For a quick lunch, top some thick slices of crusty bread with tomato sauce and melt your favourite cheese on top – Brie, Cheddar, or goat's – until it just starts to bubble. Serve with a green salad, dressed lightly with olive oil and lemon juice.

Herrings

Serve them with home-made cream cheese, curd cheese, or other soft creamy full-fat cheeses such as Explorateur, Finn, Brillat Savarin. Jewish delis always have space on their counters for creamy cheeses, and match them with salty fish, such as smoked salmon, and herring, one of my all-time loves. In a continental deli you will find smoked herring, *matjes*, very salty, but try it with a sweet-tasting black bread or soft, rich-tasting cholla spread with a full-fat cream cheese. With an *eau de vie* or schnapps you have one of the world's perfect appetizers. Search out these delis in major cities – it will be a rewarding exercise as they also stock proper pickled cucumbers, good cold fried fish, smoked salmon sliced expertly before your eyes – and if you're lucky a dead cert for the three thirty at Kempton Park while you're waiting to be served – that's if you're shopping at Panzer Delicatessen in Circus Road, St John's Wood, London NW8.

The recipes below are adapted from one of my favourite cookery writers, Evelyn Rose.

Smoked Herring Appetizer

- ◆ 2 whole matjes herrings or 4 fillets
- ◆ tomatoes
- ◆ fresh cucumber
- ◆ sweet-and-sour pickled cucumber
- ◆ lemon juice or white wine vinegar
- ◆ freshly ground black pepper
- ◆ a bunch of spring onions or 1 red-skinned onion
- ◆ chives

To serve
- ◆ black rye bread, pumpernickel or cholla
- ◆ 125 g full- or low-fat cream cheese

If you are using whole fish, remove the heads, score down the belly and remove the inside bits and pieces. Cover them with cold water and soak for 2 hours. Drain well and pat dry with paper towels, then flatten the fish skin side up, press down on the centre of the backbone, turn over the fish and carefully remove it. Any stray bones can be picked away with a sterilized pair of tweezers. Cut into fillets. Skin the fish by scraping a little of the skin from the tail end then, with the forefinger and thumb, tugging it down to the head end of the fish; it should be quite easy.

Around 30 minutes before you wish to serve it, dress the fish by cutting the fillets into 2.5-cm slices at an angle and arrange them on a serving dish with slices of tomato, skinned and seeded, fresh cucumber, skinned and seeded, and sweet-and-sour cucumber, also cut at an angle. Squeeze over the lemon juice or vinegar and grind over the black pepper before throwing on the chopped spring onion or finely sliced rounds of red-skinned onions and chives. Serve with thin slices of dark rye bread or cholla spread with a rich, creamy, full-fat cheese (or low-fat, if you must). A side dish of pickled or new green cucumbers adds to the piquancy.

Sweet and Sour or Soused Herring

Serves 6–8

- 6–8 medium fresh herrings filleted (ask the fishmonger to do this or follow the instructions for Smoked Herring Appetizer, omitting the soaking)
- salt and pepper
- 1 medium red-skinned onion, peeled and sliced finely into rounds
- 300 ml white wine or cider vinegar
- 300 ml water
- a few white peppercorns to scatter
- 1 blade of mace
- 1 bay leaf
- 2 teaspoons white or Demerara sugar
- 2 tablespoons Golden Syrup

Preheat the oven to 180°C/350°F/Gas Mark 4.

After filleting, wash, trim and scale – scrape the skin of the fish with a knife to remove the scales – then split the fish lengthways. Sprinkle them with salt and pepper and a little onion, then roll them up from the tail. Pack them side by side in a shallow casserole, with the rest of the onion, the vinegar, water and other seasonings, making sure that the liquid doesn't come over the top of the fish. Sprinkle over the sugar, spoon on the syrup and cover loosely with foil. Place in the oven until the liquid starts to bubble then turn down the heat to 150°C/300°F/Gas Mark 2 for 3 hours, after which the liquid should have reduced by half and be a dark brown. It is important that the liquid does not boil or the fish will become hard. Serve lukewarm or cool.

Note: It may be a good idea to place the casserole in a bain-marie – a large pan filled with hot water for the casserole to sit in while it cooks. This ensures an even distribution of heat.

Smoked Trout Paste on Toast with Scrambled Eggs

This is one of my favourite Sunday brunch treats, made the more enjoyable since our local Sunday Farmers' Market has a stall with the best organic smoked trout and smoked salmon I've tasted in a long time.

Serves 3–4 as an appetizer
To the weight of the skinned and flaked smoked trout fillets add an equal weight of unsalted softened (but not melted) butter and full fat cream cheese. To 200 g fish add 100 g butter and 100 g cheese or adjust the ratio to your taste. Blend to a paste, then add freshly squeezed lemon juice and a pinch or two of cayenne pepper to give an edge to the flavour – you don't want it to taste bland.

Make your scrambled eggs as usual, and serve with triangles of thinly sliced toast spread with the smoked trout paste.

Salmon Caviar

If you have a good fishmonger with whom you are on friendly terms, prise out of him lovely fresh salmon eggs to make your own caviar.

The salmon eggs (not roe) are in a slimy translucent sac, which has to be removed carefully along with any membrane. When you have released the eggs, gently wash them in cold water to remove any membrane still sticking to them – do this in a colander. Drain them well and put them in a bowl. Cover them with coarse sea salt and put a plate on top of the bowl, then put it in the fridge for at least 2 hours. Wash off the salt in several changes of water, drain well and pat dry on paper towels.

You could top your caviar, which should be made and eaten the same day to enjoy the fresh briny flavours, with finely chopped flat-leaf parsley and chives, grated lemon rind with lemon juice, and a little chopped dill.

Serve it on thinly sliced black bread, or matzos spread with cream cheese or *crème fraîche*, or perhaps with a slice of smoked salmon on the bread or matzo. It makes perfect sense to drink champagne with it.

Note: If your fingers smell fishy rub them inside half a lemon.

Christmas Blinis

If I counted how many times I'm asked each Christmas whether we stock blinis I'd be Christmas crackered by now. And why buy them when they're really simple and fun to make and taste so much better freshly baked than those ghastly rubbery things in packets? The perfect stocking filler is a non-stick blini pan about 8 cm in diameter. Those of you who prefer a heavyweight model might like a cast-iron *galettière* (you'll find these in good cookware shops such as Divertimenti or David Mellor, or via the Internet – try Lakeland Plastics, or deliaonline.co.uk). This recipe is taken from Elizabeth David's *English Bread and Yeast Cookery*.

Makes about 25 blinis
- 225 g either strong white flour or half and half buckwheat and plain strong flour
- 1 teaspoon fine sea salt
- 280 g full fat milk
- 15 g fresh yeast – ask your local baker or buy dried
- 2 large or 3 medium free-range organic eggs
- 250 g sour cream

Put the flour into a big bowl. Add the salt. Warm the milk barely to blood heat. Mix the milk and the yeast together. Separate the eggs. Stir the yolks and the cream into the milk and yeast mixture. Set aside the whites. Pour the yeast mixture into the flour and stir until you have a thick batter. If at this stage there are a few lumps in the batter it is of no consequence.

Cover the bowl, and leave it in a warm place for approximately 1 hour until the batter is spongy and bubbly.

Now whisk the egg whites to a stiff froth – as for a soufflé – and fold them into the batter. Cover the bowl again and leave the batter to rise once more, for another hour or even longer.

To make the pancakes, brush the little pan with a scrap of melted butter and set it over a medium heat. Pour in a small ladleful of batter. It will set immediately it comes into contact with the heat. In a few seconds holes appear in the top surface. Turn the blini and let it brown on the underside. Keep each one warm (with a little melted butter poured on it) in the oven while the rest are cooked. If you prefer, the blinis can be baked in the oven: just brush a baking sheet with melted butter and pour on small blobs of batter not too close together. Bake at 200°C/400°F/Gas Mark 6, flipping the pancakes over when they are nicely browned. This should only take a few minutes.

Blinis are eaten as a first – or only – course, with hot melted butter in a jug or sauceboat, cold thick sour cream in a bowl and another bowl of chopped salted herring, or caviar, or a dish of bacon rashers, or prosciutto crudo cut into strips and grilled, fried or baked in the oven while you are cooking the blinis. Or serve them with ultra-fresh *crème fraîche* and a blob of home-made Salmon Caviar (see page 68), or fresh cream cheese with herbs.

If you prefer them as a sweet course, blinis are good with cinnamon butter, maple syrup buttercream or with a little clotted cream, or even with apple purée.

Note: The batter for blinis can be kept overnight in the fridge and removed to a warm place to rise for an hour or so before it is cooked. Alternatively, provided they have not been overcooked in the first place, blinis can be reheated quite successfully. If you have made them earlier in the day or on the day before, put them on a plate, then cover with clingfilm and store them in the fridge or the larder. Bring them to room temperature before you reheat them. Put them into the oven at 180°C/350°F/Gas Mark 4, protected with buttered paper, for a few minutes.

Fricco

Traditionally made with Montasio cheese from the Friuli region of north-east Italy, these are more or less cheese crisps. They are easy to prepare and can be made with a variety of cheeses such as Coolea from Co. Cork, Sweet Milk Dunlop from Inverness, Doddington from

Northumbria, Comté from Haut Jura, Cantal from Laguiole in the Auvergne (where they're called Tuiles de Laguiole), Parmigiano Reggiano from Reggio Emilia, Asiago Vezzena (matured). As long as the cheese is hard-matured, fruity-tasting and not too oily it's OK.

Grate at least 500 g of your chosen cheese. Lightly smear a non-stick frying-pan with butter and let it melt. Spoon in 2 tablespoons of the cheese and spread it evenly into a circle of about 7 cm in diameter – you should be able to get 3 or 4 into a large pan, or you can use a blini pan. Press down to flatten them and fry until golden on both sides. Lift out the lacy crisps, pat them dry on paper towels and either keep them flat or curve them around a rolling-pin, or make a flower shape by moulding them over an inverted cup. Repeat until all the cheese is used. Serve either warm or cool, when they will taste crisp and savoury.

Another idea: make the Fricco as above, in disc form. For 4–6 people, take 100 g butter and fry 300 g assorted wild mushrooms – chanterelles, mousserons, ceps, oyster, brown cap, sprinkling over a little salt and pepper as they sizzle, and some chopped thyme. When the sizzling stops, cook the mushrooms for a minute or two longer then take them off the heat. Build up a 'mille-feuille' with a Fricco disc, then a mound of mushrooms, then a Fricco disc – say, 3 layers per portion. Serve with this simple basil-oil dressing dotted around the plate: 125 ml olive oil mixed with finely chopped basil (a handful of leaves), 1 minced garlic clove and 1 level tablespoon finely ground pine nuts.

A GUIDE TO BODY MAINTENANCE FOR SKIERS AND SPORTY TYPES

The sheer physical effort of skiing demands good eating habits with a sensible fitness routine to gain the most out of this thrilling sport.

Much as I love watching sport on TV, the programmes never point out the importance of a good diet. For instance, when you're skiing you should always have a muesli bar in your pocket to nibble – they are an instant pick-me-up at mid-morning and in the afternoon. At high altitude in extreme cold the body loses moisture and blood-sugar levels drop quickly because the air is so thin; a regular snack, such as a dried fruit and cereal bar or even chocolate, replaces the loss instantly.

Why is it so important to be aware about loss of blood sugar during strenuous physical sports and dehydration at high altitude? It's simply that our reflexes aren't at their best when this happens. It's known that 80 per cent of accidents on the pistes take place from 11 a.m. to 1 p.m. and 4 p.m. to 6 p.m., and that's why the muesli or chocolate is so important. A small chunk of hard Gruyère-style cheese, with its sweet, nutty, fruity taste, would be just as beneficial. Those skiers or sports fanatics who really push themselves to the limit should also take a vitamin B supplement to build and maintain muscle strength.

At the end of a day's skiing, exhaustion and muscle fatigue may be relieved by a gentle swim or a massage followed by a sauna. You'll feel famished, too, so a sweet milky drink, and an English-style tea, with scones, bread and butter, pastries, even a jacket potato or corn-on-the-cob will be welcome.

First thing in the morning have a good breakfast – and this means porridge, toast, fresh fruit and fruit juice, cheese or eggs, with lots of weak tea or coffee. Lunch should consist of something like vegetable soup, wholemeal bread, cheese and fresh fruit, or maybe pasta and salad, avocado pear and baked potato with cheese, lots of liquid – but no alcohol – and fresh fruit such as pineapple is especially good. Alcohol burns up energy and sugar reserves, which should be channelled into those ski-runs.

Dinner is party-time when you can let your hair down – but take alcohol in moderation: you get drunk quickly at high altitudes and the effects last longer. Even having a hot drink the next morning can trigger into action the remaining alcohol in your bloodstream, making you feel tipsy all over again.

The evening meal is an ideal opportunity to try out a traditional regional menu. Find out about the local dairy produce – it plays a big part in the day-to-day eating habits of the population. Wherever you decide to travel, and especially if you enjoy a physical sport, such as skiing, look out for local cheeses to give you strength, stamina and a taste of local produce.

The alpine region of France boasts some of the best cheeses imaginable. Look out for Beaufort (get the *alpage* or summer-milk cheese if possible): it's a grainy, fruity, hard Gruyère-style cheese. Reblochon is a semi-soft washed-rind cheese with an earthy aroma and tastes like fresh hazelnuts. Tomme de Savoie, semi-hard with a naturally ripened grey crust with patches of white and mimosa-coloured bloomy moulds, tastes flowery with a nutty sweetness. Morbier, from the Franche-Comté, is one of my favourite cheeses, with its streak of vegetal ash separating the morning and evening milks used in the cheesemaking. The taste is buttery and nutty, with a gentle aroma of fresh hay. Bleu de Gex, from Jura, or Bleu de Sassenage, from Isère, have a creamy-textured pâte with sharp blue veining – lovely when melted over baked potatoes or added to Fondue. Bleu de Termignon is an old-fashioned, dry, crumbly-textured cheese with a full and fruity flavour and naturally introduced patchy blue veining; it's only seen around the Trois Vallées in Savoie.

Raclette, the roasted-cheese dish, or Fondue are great when accompanied by a fresh green salad lightly dressed in olive oil or walnut oil (hold back on the vinegar as it does not marry well with cheese), cold meats and salami, boiled new potatoes and sweet marinated baby onions, not forgetting baby gherkins – cornichons. Vacherin, from the Haut Doubs in the Jura, is wonderfully creamy; it is matured in a spruce bark collar, which gives a 'sappy' taste to this meltingly rich confection. The baby cheeses are often baked in their box then used as a fondue (see page 20). There is a lighter version called Écorce du Sapin, but the flavour is bland. Goat's cheeses include the rarely seen St Marcellin, which is creamy and mild when young, but matures to a powerful 'gamey tasting' cheese, and Chevrotin des Aravis, the goat's milk version of Reblochon.

Switzerland produces fruity cheeses such as Appenzel, Emmentaler, Gruyère, Vacherin Mont d'Or or Fribourg, a meltingly rich and tasty Gruyère. You may also find Sbrinz, a hard cheese in the style of Parmesan; Toggenburger, which is only seen in Alpine regions; Piora, from the Italian borders; Saanen or Spalen Kase, like an Italian Grana; and Sapsago. I have just received some Sbrinz and Raclette from two young cheese-makers living in the alpine village of Engelberg, made in the traditional farmhouse style. Very tasty it was too.

Italy is the home of Fontina, a supple fruity-tasting cheese that's great for fondue; Taleggio, a soft washed-rind cheese with a powerful taste; Toma, which is like the French style *tomme* cheeses; Pannerone, rather like a white Stilton; Crescenza, a very creamy fresh-tasting cheese, good for spreading; and Gorgonzola *naturale*, an intensely flavoured blue cheese, which, when melted with a creamy cheese such as Crescenza, makes an interesting sauce to serve with Pizzocheri, the rather stolid buckwheat pasta.

Spain's hard sheep's milk cheeses are often compared with the French *brebis*, and Idiazabel, as well as a firm smoked sheep's cheese that looks rather like an elongated onion with a shiny brown skin, is delicious accompanied by *chorizo*, the strong mountain salami-style sausage, and a slice of *membrillo*, a sweet concentrated quince jelly. The blue cheeses are mind-blowing, sometimes containing a combination of cow's, goat's and sheep's milk; Picos de Europa is one of my favourites, from León in the centre of Spain: this cow's milk cheese has well-defined blue veins and is encased in vine leaves, which give it a hint of floral vegetal flavours; it combines well with a cheeseboard selection.

In Portugal look for Azeitão, a semi-soft sheep's milk cheese that uses cardoons as the coagulant. It tastes sharp and tangy. Serra da Estrela is also made with sheep's milk and cardoons; its texture is rich and creamy, the taste has a strident sharpness. Niza is an unpasteurized soft sheep and goat's milk cheese with a thin natural rind coated with pepper, olive oil and paprika. Amerelo Malpica do Tejo is another sheep and goat's milk cheese and semi-hard. Except for the very fresh, creamy cheeses, Portuguese cheese tastes tangy and lively, and rustic in style. The country's wines have a powerful bite complementary to the cheeses. But it would also be interesting to taste with them the wonderful ports available.

In Austria you will discover the mountain cheeses Bergkase and Alp-kase, the strong-flavoured Tilsiter, Stangenkase, Limburger and Edelpilz-kase, which has an almost gamey quality. The smoked cheeses are also popular, especially when served alongside large meat sausages.

Romanians follow Italian methods in cheesemaking, and the soft, mild Brinza, made from sheep's milk, is cut into cubes and preserved in brine.

Sweden and Norway produce simple hard and semi-hard cheeses, plus the more unusual Mysost, which is sweet and made with either cow's or goat's milk. In Sweden, the hard Herrgardsost is well worth seeking out, while in Norway you should try Gammelost and Pultost, and the spiced cheese, Nokkelost. However, as most cheese is made in large co-operatives, you may be disappointed in the selection, which is a shame as the farmhouse-made cheeses are altogether more interesting and satisfying.

I'd love to give you tasting notes of cheeses from India, but I'm only familiar with *paneer*, and the Middle East produces cheese similar in style to Feta, as well as very good goat's cheeses, either fresh to be used in salads or drier to be baked or grated over vegetables. My friend in Argentina, Connie, tells me she was recently on a trekking holiday in the Andes and found local hard sheep's cheeses tasting tangy and sharp, and they also had a hard Parmigiano-style cheese too.

In South Africa cheese has made quite an impact because of the emergence of their wines. We have access now to stunning white wines and their reds are drawing many fans, also the 'champagne', which, to my mind, is on a par with the real thing. I had an e-mail recently from a husband-and-wife dairy-farming team in Kenya telling me about their experiments with making cheeses in the European style. They have promised to bring me some samples when they next visit London.

In the USA you will find farmhouse-style cheeses, especially in Vermont and New York states, as well as California. Wisconsin produces Brick, soft and mild, Burmeister, Gouda style, and Hand, rather strong. Illinois has semi-soft Chantelle, Colby, which is American Cheddar, Mysost, a milder version of the Scandinavian cheese, Old Heidelberg, which is like Limburger, and Swiss. Ohio makes Coon, in the Cheddar style, Liederkranz, another version of Limburger, and Sage, a spiced Cheddar.

My friend in Australia, Will Studd, has long espoused the quality of Australian farmhouse cheeses, and whenever he visits his brother in London – he lives round the corner from my shop – he pops in to say hello, and brings with him some cheese. Most recently, he asked me to taste a soft-textured cheese aromatized with eucalyptus (rather like eating a cheese-scented throat lozenge), and a stunning blue cheese like a Roquefort, called Meredith Blue, a goat's cheese, called Edith, with white mould rind and ash coat, crumbly in the centre, its edges melting towards the rind, and a hard Cheddar style cheese from Heidi Farm. Will's book, *Chalk and Cheese*, is now available in Europe and elsewhere and is an in-depth insight into the cheeses of Australia, which, with their wines, have emerged as real stars in the making.

Fondue Savoyarde

This is the traditional French-style recipe made in an earthenware or iron casserole on a spirit stove or similar suitable heater set in the centre of your dining-table. You will also need a wooden spatula to stir the cheese, and a peppermill to add flavour as you cook. The wine to serve is a chilled Arbois or Chignin white wine from the Savoie, or a similar fresh, tangy, but not overly scented wine.

Serves 6
- *pain de campagne*, or other crusty, rustic-style bread
- 600 g Emmental de Savoie
- 400 g Beaufort *alpage* – the summer *alpage* cheeses are sweeter
- ½ Reblochon, rind removed
- 1 clove garlic
- 6 glasses dry white Savoie wine – approximately 1 bottle
- freshly ground black pepper
- 60 ml Kirsch, or Calvados or brandy

Cut the bread into bite-sized cubes. Cut the cheese into thin flakes. Cut the garlic in half and rub its open surfaces all over the sides of the casserole.

Pour the wine into the casserole and put it over a medium heat. When it bubbles, remove the pan from the heat and add the cheese bit by bit, stirring slowly with a wooden spatula. Before the cheese has melted completely, put the casserole on the table heater and continue to stir. Add a good grinding of pepper and pour in the Kirsch, still stirring. When the cheese is fully melted, turn the heat down very low.

Impale a bread cube on a fork or wooden skewer and plunge it into the fondue with a stirring motion, turning the fork to coat the bread with the cheese. The fondue must be kept moving – and if you lose your bread in it, it is traditional to pay a forfeit, which can be singing, reciting a poem . . . or removing clothing!

Note: If you want the fondue to be even richer, at the end of cooking swirl in half of a farmhouse Camembert with the rind removed. For an even tangier taste, mix in 100 g of Bleu de Gex, or a similar quantity of young Stilton.

Fonduta

This is the traditional Italian-style fondue – which, I must warn you, is very rich and rather heavy. The wine to serve might be a *vin chaud*: warm a Gamay-style wine with mulled-wine spices, thin slices of orange and apple and a splash of blackcurrant liqueur. Or choose a Piedmont white Arneis wine.

Serves 4

- 350 g Fontina from Aosta
- 200 g Toma Maccagno or Asiago Pressato (young)
- 100 g young Taleggio Valsassia
- 1 clove garlic, halved
- 80 ml creamy milk
- approximately 500 ml fruity dry white wine
- 50 g unsalted butter
- 2 very fresh medium organic free-range eggs
- sea salt and black pepper
- fresh black truffles (optional)
- 60 ml Kirsch or *grappa* (optional)

Take care while you are cooking: the mixture will curdle if it boils.

Remove all hard or textured rinds from the cheeses – but not the Taleggio unless the rind is dry – and cut them into small pieces. Rub the garlic over the casserole or fondue pan. Put the milk and butter into the pan over a medium heat and drop in a few pieces of cheese, stirring constantly, then drizzle in a little wine and mix thoroughly. Keep adding cheese and wine, stirring constantly. When you have put in all or most of the cheese and the mixture is thick and coats the back of the spoon, like thick custard, add the eggs, which you have first loosely mixed, taking care not to have the fondue mixture too hot as it may curdle. Adjust the seasoning with freshly ground black pepper and a little salt. If you wish, stir in 60 ml Kirsch or perhaps *grappa*, the Italian *eau-de-vie*, just before serving. For a touch of luxury, add grated black truffles.

Accompaniments for Fonduta include: cubes of baguette and sourdough bread, small steamed new potatoes, sticks of lightly steamed baby leeks, baby carrots, broccoli and cauliflower florets, which still have enough bite to stay intact when dipped into the molten cheese mixture.

More Fondue Ideas

Swiss Style

- 250 g Fribourg d'Estive (a fruity Gruyère)
- 100 g Emmental
- 100 g Appenzeller (a rather strong fruity-style Gruyère)
- 150 g Sbrinz (a hard Parmigiano-style cheese)

Proceed as for Fondue Savoyarde (see page 77), adding up to 500 ml wine, until the mixture coats the back of a wooden spoon like thick custard.

English Style

- 250 g Appleby's Cheshire
- 120 g Cotherstone or young Wensleydale
- 150 g medium-strength Cheddar

Proceed as for Fondue Savoyarde (see page 77), adding up to 500 ml wine, or until the mixture coats the back of a wooden spoon like thick custard. In place of the Kirsch substitute 60 ml whisky or English apple brandy.

Irish Style

- 400 g Gabriel, Desmond, or Coolea or a mixture
- 150 g young Gubbeen
- 150 g young Durrus

Proceed as for Fondue Savoyarde (see page 77), adding up to 500 ml wine, until the mixture coats the back of a wooden spoon, like thick custard. In place of the Kirsch, substitute 60 ml Irish whiskey.

Raclette

This is a cheese that melts evenly and is used to coat baked or steamed potatoes. It is quite oily and has a lovely fruity tang. You can buy table-top Raclette machines with little sliding pans to hold the cheese – useful if you are planning a party, otherwise melt the cheese under the grill. If you are holidaying in a ski resort you will also be able to buy the more traditional apparatus: you fit a quarter or half of a whole cheese on to a spiked cradle and a heating element toasts it. You scrape off the molten cheese on to your potatoes. They are very attractive, with rustic iron decoration, and make an impressive centrepiece as part of a large buffet party. I suggest you only eat Raclette in winter as it is a very hearty meal and the cheese, being rather fatty, sweats in summer.

You will need around 150 g cheese per person.

Serve the Raclette with either steamed or baked potatoes, toasted slices of sourdough or *pain de campagne* that has been brushed with white wine before the hot cheese is laid on it, assorted cold meats, ham and salami, tiny sharp-tasting *cornichon* gherkins, sweetened onions (see Braised Balsamic Onions, page 55), a green salad of mixed crisp leaves, lightly dressed with walnut or olive oil, and a squeeze of lemon. It is traditional to serve with it *vin chaud* or warmed spiced wine with the addition of blackcurrant liqueur (see page 78).

SOUPS

I'm a bit of a soup freak, and it was a toss-up as to whether I opened a soup-kitchen restaurant or a cheese shop. I remember perching as a teenager on a long bench at a refectory table in Terence Conran's first restaurant, called the Soup Kitchen, eating soup out of a small pudding basin with a wooden spoon and feeling so hip and fashionable. I thought then, and still think, soup is exciting: it's comforting, filling, and there are so many different and interesting recipes.

Fava Bean and Chick Pea Soup with Fresh Scamorze Affumicate

I ate this soup while I was in Puglia on a business trip at a restaurant set into a cliff overlooking the sea, up the coast from Bari in the picturesque town of Molfetta. I'll never forget this meal because when I ordered the fava bean soup, my companion asked, 'And will you be having the liver afterwards?' Remember *Silence of the Lambs*? We then went into Hannibal Lecter/Clarice mode, which bewildered the waiter. Afterwards we decided to walk off the huge lunch we had just eaten, and parked the car right on a small beach close to the sea. The sky was blue and the sea calmly lapping the shingle, when suddenly a rolling black cloud covered the sky. The heavens opened. We scrambled back into the car as thunder cracked, lightning flashed, and a mini-tornado practically pushed the car into the now churning sea. The drama was quite the most spectacular memory of the trip.

Fava beans are rather like split butter beans, and when cooked have a rich, creamy texture. The addition of Scamorze Affumicate, which looks like a smoked mozzarella but is closer textured, makes this soup particularly tasty. This cheese is found all over southern Italy and is used to top grilled chicken breasts, is stirred into pasta sauce or melted over vegetables, especially asparagus. As I love all sorts of pulses I have added chick peas too. Incidentally, dried pulses don't last for ever. Buy fresh ones from wholefood shops and try to get organically produced ones. I bring in my pulses from Norcia in the Perugia region of Umbria, which are probably the best in Italy. They are grown and cultivated in protected, controlled conditions and have a DOC (Denomination of Controlled Origin) status. You will need to soak the pulses the day before you want to cook them.

Serves 4
- 500 g dried split butter beans (*fave* beans)
- 250 g dried chick peas
- 2 tablespoons olive oil suitable for frying
- 100 g *pancetta*, chopped into small cubes, or streaky bacon or pork belly
- 2 carrots, scraped and diced
- 2 leeks, tough green leaves removed, trimmed, washed and finely sliced
- 1 celery stalk, strings removed and finely sliced
- 2 litres, or more, chicken or vegetable stock
- 1 bay leaf, torn
- 2 tablespoons fresh thyme leaves, finely chopped
- sea salt
- freshly ground black pepper
- 4 large potatoes, peeled, parboiled and diced
- approximately 2 tablespoons *crème fraîche* or double cream (optional)
- 2 Scamorze Affumicate, outside rind removed, cheese finely diced
- good-quality Puglian olive oil, or similar, fruity but not too powerful, to serve

Soak the *fave* beans and chick peas in separate bowls overnight. Drain and refresh them under running cold water, then pat dry. In a large heavy-bottomed casserole, heat the olive oil and fry the *pancetta*, bacon or pork until it is translucent and golden, then add the carrots, leeks and celery – add a little more olive oil if necessary. Sauté until the vegetables are becoming transparent and turning golden, add the *fave* beans and chick peas, stir through, then add the stock – at least 2 litres but have some in reserve in case you need to top it up. Drop in the torn bay leaf and the thyme, and season with salt and pepper. Bring to the boil, then simmer gently with the lid on for around 15 minutes. Put in the diced potatoes, then cook gently until everything is soft. Pass the mixture through a sieve and keep the stock, but discard the bay leaves. Mince the vegetables and beans in a food-processor or press them through a sieve with a wooden spoon, and add to the stock. Check the seasoning, but remember that the cheese has a smoky taste so take care not to oversalt it. Add more stock if the soup looks too thick. (If you want to make it creamier, add some *fromage blanc* or cream.) Reheat the soup before serving. Put a heaped teaspoon of Scamorze Affumicate into the bottom of the warm soup bowls and pour in the soup. Drizzle a circle of good-quality Puglian extra-virgin olive oil on top and serve with a crusty plain white open-textured country-style bread. Don't skim your spoon primly over the soup but dig deep into the bowl to bring up the gorgeous molten strands of cheese as well as the gutsy-tasting olive oil.

Note: To make it even more substantial, add some cooked pasta in the shape of large grains of rice.

Beetroot Borscht

Ah, beetroot. A sorry sight when it's bleeding into limp lettuce on a Sunday tea-time plate. The vinegar overwhelms any other flavour lurking innocently in the background. Luckily as a child I only met with this on visits to schoolfriends' houses, and watched as they shook globules of salad cream all over their plates in a hopeless attempt to disguise what was happening underneath. It was years later when I made Beetroot Borscht that I realized how unfairly maligned this delicious vegetable is.

Serves 4

- 1 kg young raw beetroot, with leaves, or candy beetroot if possible
- sea salt
- 2 medium-sized carrots, scraped and finely diced
- 2 litres vegetable or chicken stock
- 1–2 tablespoons tarragon vinegar
- 1 medium sweet and sour cucumber
- 1 medium New Green cucumber – from a continental deli: this is a fresh-pickled cucumber
- ¼ fresh cucumber, peeled, seeded and diced
- ½ bulb fennel, sliced with the feathery tufty bits
- 2 level tablespoons herbs – mint, tarragon, chives, dill
- 4 radishes, finely sliced
- 300 g cooked new potatoes, skinned
- 3 large hard-boiled organic eggs, shelled
- a little sugar (optional)
- 130 ml *crème fraîche*
- crushed ice cubes (optional)

Remove the stalks from the beetroot and take off the leaves. Cook the leaves in salted water for a few minutes, drain, then refresh them in cold water, pat them dry and chop them finely. Put the leaves into a tureen or large bowl. Cook the beetroot – if they are large, halve them – in boiling water until tender, then drain them. Put the cooked beetroot and the diced carrots into a saucepan with the stock, bring it to the boil and add the vinegar. Cook for 15–20 minutes until the beetroot and carrots are soft. Strain the vegetables, reserving the liquid, then sieve them or pass them through a blender. Stir the purée into the reserved broth, and pour it into the tureen. Cool completely, then cover it and place it in the fridge.

Shortly before you wish to serve the Borscht, dice the cucumbers and fennel. Finely chop the herbs. Quarter the new potatoes and the hard-boiled eggs. Taste the soup and add a little sugar and more tarragon vinegar if desired, then pop all of these ingredients into the soup. Immediately before you serve it, swirl in the *crème fraîche* and a few ice cubes.

Bloomy crust cheeses ripening in maturing room

Portuguese farmhouse cheeses

Vacherin Mont d'Or

Beaufort d'Alpage

Parmigiano Reggiano

Maconnais goat's cheeses

Selection of spring goat's cheeses (French, British, Italian)

Fresh home-made cheese   ◆   *p. 26*

Focaccia with tomatoes, creamy cheese, basil and olives ◆ *pp. 40–41*

Focaccia with Taleggio, potatoes, onions and sage ◆ *pp. 40–41*

Gorgonzola Dolce Cremificato ◆ *p. 46*

Bruschetta with Gorgonzola Dolce Cremificato, Walnuts and
Mantovana Melon ◆ *p. 46*

Cooked Ham with Fried Eggs and Melted Manchego on Toast • *p. 58*

Hamburger with Gruyère Cheese and Fried Onions • *p. 60*

Fondue ◆ *pp. 77–80*

Note: Beetroot stains everything, so use a pan specifically for the purpose. I have a black heavy-duty enamel stockpot – available from specialist utensil and cookware shops. Also wear rubber gloves or thin latex gloves (available from chemists) when handling beetroot.

Panade

A very simple rustic alpine soup.

Put 1.5 litres of boiled water (make sure this is spring water) into a saucepan with 4 cloves of garlic, minced, and 2 fresh bay leaves. Bring it to the boil. Add 125 g dry breadcrumbs and simmer for 30 minutes. Before serving add 125 ml of the freshest possible cream, 5 tablespoons of unsalted light Échire butter, 2–3 gratings of nutmeg and reheat gently. Add lots of grated Comté d'Estive or Gruyère, 200 g or more, and mix it into the soup – and put a bowl with more of the grated cheese on the table. Don't be tempted to use chicken or other stock, stick to water for the unique simple taste of this dish. For the breadcrumbs try to use a hand-baked bread that's a day or so old – it makes all the difference.

Corn Chowder

It was towards the end of August that my greengrocer next door to the shop had plump corn-cobs displayed with their husks intact. A little rummage behind the leaves revealed closely packed corn which, when squeezed, oozed its milky goodness. Sunday supper was sorted there and then. Crumbled creamy goat's cheese loosely mixed with *crème fraîche* and dropped into the chowder when you are on the point of serving is a revelation.

Serves 4
- 50 g unsalted butter
- 1 tablespoon olive oil
- 120 g *pancetta*, diced small
- 3 leeks, trimmed, cleaned and sliced
- 3 carrots, peeled and diced

- 1.5 litres, or more, spring water or stock
- 1 bay leaf
- sea salt and freshly ground pepper
- 500 g potatoes, suitable for boiling, cut into chunks
- 8–9 large fresh corn cobs, corn removed but husks retained and tied together
- 450 ml creamy milk or single cream
- 2 tablespoons chopped herbs, such as marjoram or thyme
- 1 tablespoon chopped flat-leaf parsley

In a large saucepan or heavy-duty casserole melt the butter with the olive oil. When the butter starts to turn a golden colour toss in the *pancetta* and sauté until nicely coloured and a little crisp around the edges, then slide in the leeks and carrots and sauté for 7–10 minutes on a medium heat. Next add the water or stock, bring it to the boil, pop in the bay leaf and a little salt and pepper, turn the heat down to a simmer, put on the lid and cook for 15 minutes. At this point the carrots should be soft. Strain the contents, discarding the bay leaf, and reserve the liquid in a clean saucepan. Pass the vegetables and the *pancetta* through a blender or sieve, and mix the purée into the stock. Add the potatoes, and the corn kernels with the tied husks, bring back to the boil then turn down the heat, pop on the lid and simmer for at least 20–30 minutes until the potatoes are cooked through and starting to fall apart. Add some more water or stock if the soup is too thick. Remove the husks and throw them away. Mash the potatoes a little and add the milk or cream off the heat very carefully to avoid curdling. Taste, and adjust the seasoning, then bring the soup back to a simmer. Put in the marjoram, thyme and parsley just before you serve.

Optional addition. To drop into the chowder when you've ladled it into the soup bowls: mix 250 ml *crème fraîche* with some crumbled very fresh goat's cheeses – such as 2 Innes buttons, or a fresh Sainte Maure, or a Piedmontese Caprini – and place a teaspoon of the cheese mixture on top of the soup. You might like to snip a few chives on top of the cheese.

Valle d'Aosta Layered Risotto and Fontina – Soupetta a la Cogneintze

Northern Italy produces some fine cheeses that can be compared favourably with French mountain cheeses. The Aosta region is famed for Fontina, which is similar in texture to a young Gruyère. In the old town of Cogne, right in the centre of the Gran Paradiso National Park, the beautiful scenery is complemented by some great food experiences, such as this filling soup, which is just right after a day's hiking and trekking or, closer to home, after a wet Sunday afternoon digging in the garden.

Serves 4

Take 500 g carnaroli or arborio rice and have ready about 1.5 litres of a well-flavoured chicken, beef or vegetable stock flavoured with 125 ml white wine. If you can't be bothered to make stock from scratch, substitute a bouillon cube. In a large saucepan melt 50 g (a large knob) of unsalted butter and pour in the rice and sauté for a minute or two before stirring in the stock a ladle at a time into the rice, allowing the rice to absorb each addition of the liquid. When the rice is cooked but still *al dente*, and there is still plenty of liquid to give it a soupy texture, take it off the heat. In a frying pan melt 100 g butter and fry 1-cm thick slices of baguette. When they are golden take them out of the pan and place them on paper towels to soak up any excess oil. In a casserole place a layer of the rice, then a layer of bread, then a layer of thinly sliced Fontina, or substitute Gruyère, a young Pecorino or a mild Cheddar, overlapping the slices – be generous: you will need around 250–300 g. Sprinkle a pinch of cinnamon on top, and repeat the layers. Put the casserole, uncovered, in the oven at 200°C/400°F/Gas Mark 6 until the cheese is bubbling and golden on top. Spoon the mixture into shallow serving plates and accompany it with a crisp fresh-tasting lightly chilled white wine such as Riesling.

Pumpkin Soup

The large pumpkins available around Hallowe'en make an ideal tureen, and also a clever centrepiece for an informal supper party.

Serves 6

- 4 kg pumpkin
- olive oil
- 300 g bread, diced
- 250 g *pancetta*, diced
- 1 garlic clove, minced
- 400 g cheese – Comté d'Estive or Beaufort or Gabriel, or Coolea or Fontina – thinly sliced
- 250 ml each *fromage blanc* and single cream, stirred together
- fine sea salt
- freshly ground black pepper
- 2 tablespoons chopped fresh thyme
- 1 tablespoon chopped flat-leaf parsley
- 1 tablespoon snipped chives
- garlic and herb ciabatta bread

Preheat the oven to 180°C/350°F/Gas Mark 4. Slice off the top of the pumpkin to make a decent lid. Scoop out the seeds and stringy bits, leaving the fleshy sides intact. Heat a tablespoon of olive oil in a frying pan and put in the diced bread, with the *pancetta* and the garlic. Fry until they are crisp and golden, turning regularly. Then layer them in the pumpkin shell with the cheese until you reach the top. Season the cream mixture with a little fine sea salt and freshly ground black pepper, then stir in the thyme, and pour it into the pumpkin. Pop on the lid. Lightly rub the outside of the pumpkin with olive oil before you slide it on to a baking sheet and place it on the middle shelf of the oven. Bake for 1–1½ hours. Test after around an hour to see if the pumpkin flesh has softened sufficiently – you don't want the outside shell to collapse! Take it out of the oven and remove the lid. Stir the cooked creamy middle carefully, scooping some of the pumpkin flesh into the soup. Check for seasoning and scatter over the flat-leaf parsley and chives before serving. Accompany with the ciabatta, toasted and buttered.

Note on cheeses: Comté and Beaufort are from the Savoie region of eastern France, Gabriel is from Co. Cork and made in the Swiss style using traditional copper vats by one of the nicest cheesemakers I know,

Bill Hogan. Their fruity grainy texture and rich buttery taste are perfect for melting. The Northumbrian cheese Doddington, as well as its more supple sister Cuddy's Cave, is a cross between Cheddar and Gouda with a distinctive fruity-salty tang, as the grazing areas are about twelve miles from the coast. The Coolea is an Irish-style Gouda. You can, of course, experiment with Italian cheeses, such as Fontina or Asiago (young), or a similar Spanish cheese such as a young Mahón or Manchego.

Venetian Onion Soup

Italian soups are the business: they're thick, full of flavour and often with cheese that melts into a molten stringy mass. Delicious. The onions from the Veneto region are famous for their flavour and sweetness, and a wintry soup such as this is a warming welcome home – a mini-hearth in a bowl. If you don't want to take the long route when making the stock – which is well worth all the effort, I can assure you – then cans of beef or chicken consommé or vegetable stock cubes can be substituted, but don't add too much salt.

Serves 6

FOR THE STOCK

- 2 meaty beef bones, fat removed
- 1 veal marrow bone
- 1 kg beef shin or topside
- 1 cooked chicken carcass (optional)
- 2 carrots, scrubbed
- 2 onions, skins left on
- 1 stick celery
- 1 large leek, washed and split in half
- 1 teaspoon sea salt
- 6–7 black peppercorns
- bouquet garni, with bay-leaf, thyme, parsley stalks tied together

- 160 g unsalted butter
- 1 kg firm onions, peeled and finely sliced
- 125 ml Valpolicella or similar fruity red wine
- 2 tablespoons chopped thyme

TO SERVE
- 6 slices baguette, about 1 cm thick
- olive oil
- 300 g Fontina or Asiago Pressato, or Gruyère style cheese, finely shredded

Heat the oven to 180°C/350°F/Gas Mark 4, and roast the beef and veal bones until they are brown (this way, the soup will have a lovely brown colour). Set them to one side. Take a very large saucepan and put in it the bones with the shin or topside – or a combination of both – and the chicken carcass, if you are using one. Cover with water. Bring it to the boil, and skim off any scum until it ceases to appear. Then add the carrots, onions (with the skin on), the celery and the leek. Top up the water until it covers everything and bring the pan back to the boil. Then turn down the heat low, add the salt, the peppercorns and the bouquet garni, put on the lid and cook gently for 2 hours. Take it off the heat and strain the soup, which should be a rich dark colour and well flavoured. If you like, you could purée the vegetables (removing the onion skin) and stir them into the soup to thicken it. Discard the chicken carcass – and maybe you know a dog who would like beef and veal bones. You could add the meat to a fricassée with potatoes – or why not concoct something inventive?

To finish the soup, heat the butter in a frying pan until it is foaming, then sauté the onions until they are a deep golden brown but have not caramelized excessively. With a slotted spoon, drop them into the soup. Taste and adjust the seasoning, then bring it back to the boil. Add the wine, stir, and let it heat through. Just before serving, sprinkle over the thyme.

To serve, brush the baguette slices with olive oil and put them into a preheated oven at 200°C/400°F/Gas Mark 6 until they are golden. Place a piece in each soup bowl with a heap of the cheese, and pour over the bubbling hot soup.

SALADS

My Mozzarella di Bufala and Tomato Salad

June to the end of September is a time for tomatoes. Of course we see them all year, but it is particularly during these months that the taste, smell and juicy texture are best. There is a man selling many different varieties of tomatoes at my local Sunday farmers' market. He has a table piled high with tomatoes of varying shapes and sizes, from the red-green Sardo and Ciliegia vine to the Perino and juicy San Marzano, as well as English salad tomatoes. He sells out within an hour or two.

Slow-roast some cherry tomatoes on the vine in a little good Puglian or your favourite well-flavoured olive oil, adding shavings of *estrattu di Pomodoro* – the dark concentrated 'cake' of tomatoes made in Sicily – or a very thick concentrated tomato sauce. Keep the temperature of the oven low – 140°C/275°F/Gas Mark 1 – and let them cook gently overnight on the bottom shelf. The result will be a deeply mellow sweet and savoury flavour. Let the tomatoes cool to room temperature and slice the freshest buffalo mozzarella you can lay your hands on. The cheese should not be too cold but not warm either. As your knife passes through the cheese the milk should gently ooze out of it. If you wish a more rustic look, break the cheese into chunky pieces. Over this scatter roughly torn basil leaves (green or purple or a mixture of both) and black pepper you have crushed coarsely with a pestle in a mortar. Drink a crisp light Frascati with it – and this is me sitting on my terrace on a rare balmy summer's day.

Summer tomatoes should be naturally sweet; you may like to add a teaspoon of sugar to them to intensify the flavour, but be cautious.

Buffalo Mozzarella

The Italian word *mozzare* means to cut (when the heated and stretched curd is then cut into ball-size pieces), and whenever you are able to lay your hands on the more artisan cheeses rather than the factory-made ones you will notice several differences. First, the milk used in artisan cheeses is fresh, not dried or frozen, and this will be evident from the oozing translucent quality of the milk as the cheese is sliced open. Next, a hand-made cheese is soft and pliable; it also has a sort of shredded look inside, from the many fine layers achieved after the cheese has been stretched. The milk moistens the layers, giving the taste and texture a fresh, chewy, light, lactic quality with no hint of rubbery blandness.

The town of Battipaglia in Campania, just below Naples, is the original grazing zone for the Indian white buffalo, introduced to the Italian countryside when the Italian naval fleet returned from their early adventures in Asia. In the past, the marshy humid plains could not be farmed because a plague had contaminated all of the land. However, the buffalo survived and were put to use as beasts of burden. Their gentle nature made them an invaluable asset to the almost destitute local smallholders, and their milk formed part of the staple diet for the community. However, it was only when the farmers took their cheese as a gift to the King of Naples that its delicacy and charm were recognized and it metamorphosed into a rich man's feast. Whenever possible, buy hand-made fresh buffalo-milk mozzarella for its simple purity. Also, if you have a sweet myrtle bush in your garden, wrap some of its thin branches when they are in blossom around a very fresh mozzarella to aromatize and add a hint of its flavour.

Morning-after-the-night-before Lunchtime Salad

A reviving dish that is full of vitamins. Artichokes are good for the liver, salty capers and cheese replace the mineral and protein losses incurred by over-imbibing, while lemon and olive oil cleanse the system.

- a big chunky slice of sourdough bruschetta, smeared with olive pâté and baked until golden
- watercress, washed and picked over, tough stalks removed
- flat-leaf parsley, chopped
- baby capers, either salted, which you must rinse and drain, or in oil
- fresh salty cheeses, such as sheep's milk feta, fresh goat's milk Crottin or a cow's milk triple cream
- wood-roasted artichokes (from a good deli)
- green olives, stoned
- roasted vine tomatoes drizzled with chilli-spiked olive oil and a squeeze of lemon juice
- freshly ground black pepper

Take your warm bruschetta and heap on it the watercress and flat parsley, scatter over the capers and lay on the cheese, artichokes, olives and tomatoes. Sprinkle with freshly ground black pepper.

Goat's Cheese Salad with Walnuts

The Loire region, situated below Brittany, boasts some of the best goat's cheeses in France, such as Crottin de Chavignol and Sainte-Maure-de-Touraine. Also lovely fresh, tangy small goat's cheeses, such as Innes buttons, are produced in Britain. In Scotland there is a favourite of mine called Califer, from Moray, Inverness. In Avon, you will find Mary Holbrook's goat's milk pyramid cheeses, which are best eaten in summer and early autumn. They should not be tampered with – enjoy them simply with a slice of crusty bread and a glass of chilled white Sancerre.

For a quick, easy lunch or first course at dinner, choose a selection of green salad leaves – some soft, some bitter, some crisp. Finely chop a mixture of flat-leaf parsley, chervil, thyme leaves and chives, and toss them with the salad leaves. Pan-fry some roughly chopped walnuts or pine nuts until they are lightly golden then toss them into the salad. Dress the salad with a little walnut oil or a not-too-strong olive oil. Slice or cube your chosen goat's cheese and place it on top of the salad. (If it is very fresh, crumble it lightly over the leaves.)

Soft Sheep's Milk Cheese with Olive Salad

The fresh, sweet creaminess of the cheese, matched with the olive and caper salad, has a refreshing appeal especially when it is accompanied by a smoky spicy Provençal or Béarnais rosé wine.

- 200 g very fresh soft sheep's milk cheese
- 200 g sheep's milk ricotta, such as Sairass from the Piedmont, or any fresh soft cheese of your choice
- 200 g of black and green Provençal olives. (Don't buy the stoned variety – *please*!)
- 1 heaped tablespoon tiny salted capers, washed, dried and chopped
- 2 heaped tablespoons chopped flat-leaf parsley
- 1 tablespoon finely chopped red-skinned onion, or spring onion or shallot
- 1 clove garlic, minced
- 1 tablespoon chopped thyme
- 1 tablespoon chopped rosemary
- around 4 tablespoons extra-virgin olive oil, to mix

Mash the cheese with a light hand and heap it into a serving bowl – light hand means not, as some may say, 'giving it some'.

Stone the olives, chop them finely and mix them with the capers and the parsley. Stir the onion, garlic, thyme and rosemary into the extra-virgin olive oil and blend well. Fold it into the olive mixture. If you can leave the olive salad to marinate for an hour or two all the better. Serve it in a separate bowl alongside the cheese and have plenty of toasted bruschetta, ciabatta or Piadina bread to use as a scoop.

Scallops with Walnut Vinegar Glaze and Fresh Sheep's Milk Cheese and Walnut Salad

A smart, stylish creation for an impressive appetizer. The walnut vinegar is a revelation and I have been singing its praises as a dressing for salads as well as adding to meat and fish dishes.

Serves 4

- ◆ 12 large scallops, with or without the coral
- ◆ 3–4 tablespoons olive oil
- ◆ 4 tablespoons walnut vinegar
- ◆ freshly ground black pepper
- ◆ mixed salad leaves – for example, rocket, watercress, radicchio
- ◆ 2–3 tablespoons walnut oil
- ◆ 1 fresh sheep's milk cheese or mixed-milk cheese such as Robiola di Langhe, without rind
- ◆ 1 tablespoon salted capers, washed and drained
- ◆ 100 g lightly toasted walnuts, roughly crushed

Pan-fry the lovely, plump, juicy scallops in the olive oil until they have just caramelized around the edges – just a few minutes – then remove them from the pan and pat them dry on paper towels. Put them to one side and de-glaze the pan with a few splashes of walnut vinegar, then drizzle this sauce over the scallops. Grind over a little black pepper.

Tear the salad leaves roughly into shreds. Drizzle over the walnut oil and loosely toss with your hands. Crumble over the cheese, then toss in the capers and walnuts. Serve the salad on the side rather than on the plate with the scallops.

To make it a more substantial meal, serve the scallops with potatoes mashed with *fromage blanc*, and leave the cheese out of the salad.

More Quick Salad Ideas

- ◆ Assemble in a bowl some chargrilled baby artichokes (from a good deli), cubed feta, chopped fresh mint, finely chopped Salerno or Amalfi lemons – use the whole lemon – fresh-shelled baby peas, tossed in extra-virgin olive oil with a grinding of black pepper. Mix them together and pile on to a large crisp iceberg lettuce leaf. Serve with toasted bruschetta rubbed with garlic oil to use as a scoop.

- ◆ Mix cubed Beaufort cheese and frazzled *pancetta lardons* into soft green *mâche* (lamb's lettuce) leaves that have been coated in walnut oil with a little walnut vinegar.

- Place some salad leaves – for example, sorrel, rocket, lamb's lettuce – in a bowl with a dressing of fresh Cabécou de Rocamadour cheese (a small medallion-sized soft creamy goat's cheese with a thin natural rind) blended to a cream with walnut oil and crushed black peppercorns, and toss.

- Try rocket, sorrel and watercress topped with slivers of Gorgonzola *dolce* and a dressing of mashed baby capers (use the salted ones, but wash and dry them before use) and a couple of de-salted 'raw' anchovies (or anchovy fillets in oil) creamed together with extra-virgin olive oil and coarsely ground black pepper.

- Brush Crottin de Chavignol goat's cheese with olive oil and scatter over some peppercorns, then grill it. Serve it on a bed of leaves dressed in walnut oil and walnut vinegar with a scattering of roasted broken walnuts.

- Wrap Crottin in a paper-thin slice of *prosciutto* and grill it, turning, for about 5 minutes. Set it on a slice of toasted ciabatta rubbed with olive oil and spread thinly with mashed black olives. Serve with cherry tomatoes slow-roasted in olive oil with aromatic herbs (see page 95).

A Travelling Tale

IN SEARCH OF OSSAU

Hidden away in the rugged beauty of the Pyrénées-Atlantiques are cheese-maturing caves nurturing their small boulders of golden cheese. When curiosity finally got the better of me I went in search of the rare and delicious Ossau cheese. Now there is Ossau and Ossau – and the one I get is the farmhouse-made cheese stamped with the farmer's brand and the maturer's number. Not for me a factory-made offering: I want to taste the *terroir*, the farmer's toil and the maturer's skill in every bite.

We all want to find the perfect hiding place for a summer idyll, and I've been trying for most of my adult life, Michelin red book in one hand, map in the other, zigzagging around Europe, off the beaten track, up mountain passes, down gorges, broken down and out of petrol in the most out-of-the-way places. But still I want to seek out that special place, and taste the simple luxury of home cooking.

As ever, for me it all comes down to cheese. If I'm offered a good cheeseboard I know I'm in safe hands. In south-west France, racing down from Toulouse on the main road to Tarbes, then on to Pau is easy enough, with hills and greenery all around, the odd ruin to remind us of the massacre of the Cathars in the twelfth century. In fact, there's a cheese called Cathare, which is made not far from Carcassonne: it's a goat's cheese shaped rather like a saucer with a black ash coat and the cross of the Cathars imprinted on it. It's delicious, with a lingering fruity tang and soft, yielding texture. We drove along empty roads, through the rugged, wild landscape, listening to French pop music and, for some unknown reason, Leo Sayer's old hit 'I'm Going to Rio, Rio de Janeiro'.

Pau is rather like Marlborough in Wiltshire, with pinky-beige stone buildings glowing in the late-afternoon sun. There's a mass of history here, and it is linked to Britain through the Church and a royal connection in the Middle Ages, which is evident in the street names. The complex layout of winding cobbled streets, majestic squares and walkways with elegant boutiques did nothing for my map-reading skills, and Danny had a few choice words for me as we passed the same group of shops yet again. And then, by sheer chance, we found Gabriel Bachelet's cheese shop at 24 rue Maréchal Joffre: a small shop, with open shelves, in which the personality of the owner is expressed in the decoration and display. It is difficult to explain and describe this, but the words 'happy', 'welcoming' and 'relaxed' come to mind. And Monsieur Bachelet is an authority on the farmhouse-made Ossau cheese, and my guide to the Holy Grail. His shop manager let us snoop around downstairs before handing us a rough sketch of the way to the hotel where we were to stay. It was in Gan, just outside Pau. We were instructed to meet Monsieur Bachelet the next morning at nine o'clock in the car park of the Jurançon wine co-op on the main road not far from the hotel. I was starting to feel excited: I'd planned this for a year and now I was going to meet the family who make the wonderful Ossau cheese.

Gan is a few kilometres from Pau, on the Saragosse road. It is a pleasant drive through hamlets where spindly trees line the route. However, it was getting dark, and the crude map, with my lack of sense of direction, threatened to leave us stranded in the middle of nowhere. Suddenly I saw the cheese co-op, then the Jurançon wine co-op. I told Danny to go next right – just in time – then under the bridge and follow the track up to the Auberge l'Horizon. We all want a special place to stay, nestling in the hillside, away from the madding crowd and not listed in Michelin – and this is it. I'm giving you an address you'll thank me for. It's perfect, with an unspoilt view for miles – and, on that occasion, it had the added attraction of a bird singing a wild unrelenting tune in the tree outside our bedroom. No locks on any doors and no designer furnishings and fripperies. Bliss.

As the evening was still and warm we ate on the terrace where our new friends, the shaggy mountain shepherd dog and the owners' cat, sat beside us as if to make us feel part of the family. The evening was a perfect backdrop to the faint hum of cicadas. There was a stillness all around us and we watched the sky turn from a glowing ember to indigo as night closed in. Somewhere in the distance we heard the staccato bark of a lone dog. The food was ambitious but well prepared, from the plate of seasonal salad vegetables with a basil sorbet, to the red mullet wrapped in Serrano ham, then the various sheep's milk puddings from junket to mousse to *fromage frais*. I resisted the temptation to try the cheese, as the next day would be spent tasting a great deal.

In the morning we were joined by Gabriel Bachelet's daughter, Christine, and we went to meet him at the co-op as arranged before making our way to Sévignacq-Meyracq, thirty kilometres away on the winding D934, with its steep rocky outcrops, tunnels chipped out of rock, streams rushing alongside, to where the Bonnaserre family farm their fifty sheep. If you have travelled through France you will have passed through hamlets like this carved out of the mountainside, quietly going about their business, revealing little of their life. We passed over a narrow bridge, wound our way up a road, then a track, and were at the Bonnaserre farm. Roger, the father, was amiable and welcoming, his wife Marie-Thérèse (affectionately called Josette) had a smile to melt the hardest heart. Their son Jean-Pierre, with piercing black eyes, well-defined dark eyebrows and a taut muscular body, looked serious and intense, while Michel, his younger brother, rotund and rather shy, preferred to stay in the background. The sheep had just been to the milking shed, and were waiting in the barn to make the trek up to the higher pastures: 5, 6 and 7 July are the days allocated for transhumance, when all the cattle and flocks leave the heat of the valley for the cooler lush mountain pastures. This is a time when animals have priority on the roads, and they are led by the local families, their friends and dogs, while carts pulled by sturdy-looking mountain ponies are laden with supplies to sustain them on their way. Once they reach the high pastures, herdsmen and shepherds look after the animals and live in little stone or wooden huts. Milking and cheesemaking sheds are accessible by road or track so that the cheese can be collected and taken to the maturing caves. The Bonnaserres had three sheepdogs, which drove the sheep through the gate and on to the upper pastures with an intelligence and cunning that made human assistance redundant.

Now we could concentrate on making the cheese. There is a marked difference between cheese made from milk that has been brought a few yards to the dairy from the milking shed, and industrial-style cheeses that have been made with milk collected from several farms then transported to the *laiterie* to be processed in large vats with mechanical skimmers and shredders. We had approximately 200 litres of milk to make a maximum of eight cheeses. The milk from twelve or thirteen sheep makes a 2 kg cheese – so now you know why sheep's milk cheese is expensive. Three large pans were sitting on gas burners in the cheesemaking shed, heating the milk up to 30°C/86°F. Then the heat was turned off, and the rennet added to coagulate the milk. A cloth was placed over each pan and we waited for around twenty minutes before a long-pronged fork was inserted to separate the curds into small pieces before the pans were covered again and left to cool to just warm. By then the curds had dropped to the bottom, and Josette and Michel plunged their hands into the pans to gather them up and drop them into moulds. First, though, Josette took a saucer, spooned out some of the warm curds and gave them to me. The taste transported me back to my childhood, when my mother made junket, and I'd perch myself on the kitchen table to eat it while *Listen with Mother* was on the radio. Could I have a go at gathering up the curds? I asked. Josette was pleased that I was taking such an interest in what she thought of as one of her daily chores.

I washed my hands and arms then lowered them gently into the liquid. The small cheesemaking room was already hot – the outside temperature must have been in the eighties, and the heat of the pan fanned my face. My cheeks turned beetroot red. My hands reached to the bottom of the pan where I found the curds, brought them together and carefully lifted them out of the whey. '*Vite, vite*,' urged Josette, and guided me a few steps to the mould. She told me how to press down the curd so that the excess moisture would drip out of the tiny draining holes around the mould. Then long thin needles were inserted in the cheese to push out more whey. I was told that this sort of draining process is used for Cheshire cheese too. When as much of the whey as possible had been expelled the cheese was slid out of the mould, and fine muslin was placed inside as a lining. Then the Bonnaserre wooden stamp was pressed into the bottom of the cheese before it was popped back into the muslin-lined mould and covered over. A china plate went on top and it was left to cool and dry out before being taken to the cellar. The cheeses would not be salted for another day or two – they had to be dry before being handled.

The whey released from the cheese is fed to the pigs and chickens, and the whey left in the pan with bits of curd is heated up again to 32°C/90°F then left to cool down for an hour; the resulting ricotta is placed in a cloth and hung up to drain.

When all eight cheeses were finished, we hosed down the dairy and walked out into the dazzling midday sun, the light breeze a welcome relief. Then Roger Bonnaserre took me on a farm tour. First he showed me the milking parlour, then the piggery, and the hens – running madly around – their tufts of feathery hair reminded me of Rod Stewart. Next there were rabbits, and finally we went into the large barn where the huge shaggy mountain dog was lying on a straw bed – and there were four magpies in a cage. Roger explained that they attack the chickens so he lays traps to catch them then releases them away from the farm.

We wandered back to the farmhouse as the clock struck midday, which meant it was time for an hour away from work and lunch. But first Roger opened a bottle of Jurançon wine and Josette spooned out some ricotta from the crock in the fridge, and we sat around the large kitchen table, sipping the cool, delicately scented wine and enjoying the silky smooth naturally sweet taste of the cheese. We laughed and chatted, and their easy familiarity made me feel very much part of their family. The pressure cooker on the old range hissed and rumbled, its contents emitting a most delicious aroma.

It was time for us to journey on up the mountain and leave the Bonnaserre family to their well-earned lunch. Gabriel was taking us to see Monsieur Laborde, known to his friends as Jeannot, who matures all the cheeses in this area in his caves set in the mountain, and if we were to get there in time for lunch, we had to press on.

We drove through dramatic scenery, winding our way along a route beside the Gave d'Ossau river to L'Hôtel Biscau in the mountain range of Pic Biscau. The hotel-restaurant is a stopping-off point for hikers and tourists wanting to explore the area, and Jeannot Laborde has carved out for himself a lucrative business in maturing cheese, selling it at the roadside and providing a watering-hole for hungry travellers. We sat down with Jeannot, and a large plate of Bayonne ham and potatoes with salad and another of Ossau cheese with the traditional black cherry conserve and bread were set before us. We washed them down with a potent local wine. After a couple of glasses Gabriel Bachelet showed that he has a mischievous sense of humour and goaded Jeannot about his appearance: how could such an important man with such a successful business dress so badly, and wasn't it about time he got some new hair? (Jeannot was wearing a rather ill-fitting hairpiece and he took this all in good part.)

I was getting impatient to see the caves and asked Jeannot if he would show me around personally. As he led me around his empire he changed swiftly from amiable charmer to serious businessman. There were two different types of cave. The first was large and modern, with temperature controls and modern facilities for maturing cheeses. Row upon row of shelves reached up thirty feet or more, filled with cheese. Hundreds of thousands of pounds worth of stock. Then he led me across the courtyard to a stone building that opened into a cave. This, he said, was for the artisan-made cheeses, like the Bonnaserres', and maturing was carried out in natural conditions, without the aid of extra cooling systems or humidity. The cave's walls and stone floor were wet, and the shelving was of old seasoned wood. The atmosphere was quiet and calm, with only the sound of dripping water seeping out of the stone walls. The glow of low-wattage lights made it a spooky yet romantic setting as we walked down the aisles, stopping every so often to inspect cheeses, stroke them, or tap their crust, or breathe in their aroma. Jeannot showed me how he treated the fresh cheeses, by rubbing sea salt (the grey unwashed kind) into the rind, and how they changed as the maturing process progressed. The crusts took on a deep ochre, their mimosa moulds flecked with white, becoming darker as they aged, giving them a rock-like appearance. Gabriel took a cheese off a shelf and said, 'Look, here is one of the Bonnaserre cheeses,' and handed it to me. I could see the familiar BR imprint and it looked half mature, its dark ochre rind developing beautifully. 'You will have this cheese in time for Christmas,' said Gabriel, and he asked Jeannot to make sure it was kept in tip-top condition for me so that my customers in London could experience the most delicious cheese in south-west France. Jeannot was amazed that I sold these cheeses in London, as few of the real artisan varieties ever leave the region. Then Gabriel interrupted: 'Get a new hairpiece, Jeannot, and visit Patricia's shop in London with me.'

It was now mid-afternoon and Gabriel, his van filled with cheese from Jeannot, was ready to return to his shop in Pau. This is where we had to say goodbye to him too – I wanted to carry on up the mountain road to the summit, Col du Pourtalet, on the border with Spain. 'Had a good day?' enquired Gabriel.

'Unforgettable,' was all I could say.

'What are you up to tonight, then?' he asked.

'Well, after all this rustic simplicity I'm off to have dinner at the three-star Michel Guérand Les Prés d'Eugénie at Eugénie-les-Bains.'

He laughed and said, with a twinkle in his eye, 'Don't forget to try the cheeses there – I supply them and they're the best. I'll phone and tell them to give you special attention!'

It had been a wonderful experience that seemed over too quickly, and the evening . . . well, that was unbelievable too, but you'll have to wait for that story . . .

I couldn't end this piece without a very special recipe for Fig Jam to serve alongside Ossau cheese. This is a treasured scrap of paper given to me by Eric as a gift from his grandmother. She kindly sent us some jars of her fig jam one year, and I went all lyrical when I tasted it. Its sweetness, with a hint of astringency, is a perfect foil for the Ossau cheese, and although it works well with commercially bought fruit, I expect the plump juicy figs from her orchard picked and placed straight in the preserving pot still warm from the sun make a vastly superior jam.

La Confiture de Figues – Grandmère Marie-Louise

Take a preserving pan or saucepan used specifically for jam. Wash and pat dry 2 kg ripe purple figs, then cut them into halves or quarters and mix with 1.5 kg sugar. Turn into the mixture 2 large lemons, finely sliced, and 125 ml wine vinegar. Bring to the boil, then simmer for 45 minutes. Drop in a split vanilla pod. Continue to cook until you think the jam is thick enough. To test whether it is ready, place a spoonful on a saucer: if it sits in a mound and doesn't spread too much, it's done. Anyway, as the mixture cools it will thicken naturally. French jam is not like our English-style jam: it tastes more of the fruit with the sweet and tart flavours intact – and this is what we want to achieve in this recipe. Have ready 6–8 200 g sterilized jars to fill with the jam once it is cool enough to pot up. Place a circle of waxed paper on top when the jam is completely cool before sealing with a lid.

POLENTA AND POTATOES

Polenta with Cheese

Try cooking polenta from scratch. Use the more rustic yellow polenta with the husk included or the very fine white polenta.

You will need 500 g of polenta to about 2.5 litres of plain spring water. Cook it slowly, as you would porridge, stirring to prevent lumps forming. (To help stop the mixture sticking to the saucepan put a – washed! – pebble in the pot.) When it is thick and creamy stir in at least 150 g of fragrant Fontina or young Gruyère-style cheese and a grating of nutmeg. Taste and season, if you like, with salt and pepper. Serve, with a spoonful of Mostarda (sweet preserved fruits in mustard syrup) or a fruit and nut chutney, grilled lamb cutlets, or chunky sausages.

Another polenta idea: Add a mixture of Fontina and Taleggio (75 g of each) to the cooked polenta and serve with 250 g wild mushrooms you have sautéd in butter with garlic and chopped fresh sage.

Smacafam

I love this name – it means to appease one's hunger in the Italian Trentino dialect. Prepare it a day before, then reheat it in the oven, and you have a real winter warmer. The basic constituent is polenta which, rather like sun-dried tomatoes, has been over-hyped to the point of cliché, but it is one of my favourite ingredients. It is specially good with cheese, becoming soft and gloopy like a good porridge, and has a particular affinity with lamb, beef and chicken or, even better, fried wild mushrooms.

- 2½–3 litres spring or filtered water, brought to the boil
- 500 g polenta with husk, organic if possible
- 2 teaspoons sea salt

FOR THE FILLING
- olive or sunflower oil
- 2 large onions, peeled and thinly sliced
- 200 g fresh soft *pancetta*, cut into small cubes
- 250 g Italian meaty sausages, or fresh Bologna sausages, or any continental-style sausages
- 2 large cloves garlic, peeled and chopped
- 250 g grated young Asiago, or Montasio, or mild-flavoured semi-hard cheese, like young Gruyère or Cotherstone – even a melting one, like Crescenza or mozzarella
- 120 g grated Grana or young Parmesan

Half fill a large saucepan with water and bring it to the boil. Take a metal bowl or another saucepan that fits snugly on top without touching the water. Before placing the bowl on the pan, pour in approximately 2½–3 litres of boiling water, and then, in a fine stream, pour in the polenta with the salt, whisking with a large wire balloon whisk in the same direction all the time until the polenta is completely blended with the water. Cover the bowl with foil and seal it smoothly, then place it on the saucepan of simmering water, making sure that it does not come into contact with the water. Let it cook for 1½ hours, ensuring that the water in the saucepan is at a rolling boil on a medium heat. You may need to top up the water from time to time. Stir the mixture with a flat wooden spoon or rubber spatula occasionally, right down to the bottom of the bowl, and reseal the foil each time. After the allotted time the mixture should be thick and creamy, like a smooth porridge, and it should not taste uncooked.

While the polenta is cooking, turn the oven to 180°C/350°F/Gas Mark 4 if you want to eat the Smacafam straight away, and make the filling. In a large heavy frying-pan heat enough oil to coat the base of the pan. Fry the onions and the *pancetta* until golden and translucent. Remove and place on paper towel to soak up some of the oil. If necessary, add a little oil to the pan and fry the sausages until they are brown, crisp and caramelized. Remove and keep them warm, then fry the garlic for a minute or two to soften. Take it out and mix it with the onions.

Finely chop the cooked sausages and stir them into the onion mixture. Take a terrine or Pyrex baking dish and oil it lightly. Pour some polenta, about a centimetre deep, into the bottom, then sprinkle over half of the cheese, and cover with half of the filling. Repeat, ending with a layer of polenta. Top with the Grana or Parmigiano Reggiano.

Leave to cool, then cover and refrigerate overnight, or bake immediately for around 35 minutes and serve. The dish improves if it is kept overnight before baking.

If using a terrine you may prefer to unmould the Smacafam after refrigerating, and cut it into portions (dip the blade of the knife into hot water and wipe it dry each time before cutting as this will help you to cut clean slices). Slide them on to a lightly oiled baking sheet and place it in the oven at 220°C/425°F/Gas Mark 7 for 10 minutes or so, dusting over some more Parmigiano Reggiano or Grana before serving.

Note: If you don't want to use sausages, try a mixture of fried wild mushrooms and brown cap mushrooms instead.

Mashed Potatoes with Fromage Blanc and Parmigiano Reggiano

With the weekly Farmers' Markets appearing all over London as well as across the country, at last we can have the freshest possible vegetables even if we have to scrub them a bit to get the soil off. This simple dish goes well with a robust stew or delicate chicken breasts poached in white wine.

- 1 kg potatoes suitable for steaming
- 120 ml creamy organic milk
- 120 g best-quality unsalted butter
- 150 g *fromage blanc* or *fromage frais*, low- or full-fat (your choice)
- coarse-grained sea salt
- 100 g finely grated Parmigiano Reggiano

Steam the potatoes in their skins until they are cooked through. Remove the skins and 'dry out' the potatoes if they are rather wet in a large saucepan over a medium heat. Add the milk and butter and heat through but don't let the milk boil. Mash the potatoes well, giving them a good thorough beating, then add the *fromage blanc* or *fromage frais* and some salt. Pile the potatoes into a bowl, sprinkle over the Parmigiano Reggiano, then flash under the grill to colour the cheese a golden-brown.

Aligot

In Britain our potatoes are perfect for cooking with cheese. The Auvergne region of France produces a few hard cheeses that resemble some of our traditional varieties, such as matured Cheddar, Lancashire and Caerphilly. If you are a purist you may disagree, but I think we can have a good stab at re-creating this weirdly wonderful stretchy cheese and potato dish. The Auvergnats make a great display of pulling the mixture as high as possible with a huge ladle. After every few turns in the vast cauldron bubbling away on the stove the ladle is lifted up with the smooth mixture clinging to it until it snaps back into the saucepan. This ensures that the mixture acquires smoothness and elasticity. With *jambon de Bayonne*, or similar smoked cured ham, a variety of salami, balsamic onions, lightly steamed green beans and a green salad, you have a filling, satisfying dish.

First: know your cheese. Aligot uses a very fresh Tomme d'Auvergne or Tomme de Cantal, a week-old curd before it has developed a crust or the smooth, mellow, nutty flavours of the aged cheese. I only ever bring it into La Fromagerie for special orders as it has a short life and must be used immediately.

However, we can get round this problem. Very young Lancashire (Shorrocks is a good one), Caerphilly or Wensleydale are good substitutes, as long as the Lancashire or Wensleydale have just been made, and the Caerphilly is as young as possible (a young Gorwydd would work). Have a go at making Aligot for a casual lunch or dinner party and get everyone to lift the ladle (or a large wooden spoon) to see how high they can go. The French have such simple ways of entertaining themselves.

Serves 8
- ◆ 2 kg floury potatoes
- ◆ sea salt
- ◆ 125 g unsalted Charente butter (from western France: the northern French butters are far too fatty) or any light, sweet-tasting butter
- ◆ 200 g cream, unpasteurized if possible
- ◆ 1–2 cloves garlic, peeled and minced
- ◆ 500 g very fresh week-old Lancashire or Wensleydale, or very young light-textured Caerphilly, crumbled

Steam the potatoes in their skins, then peel and purée them, adding a little salt. In a good-sized saucepan, heat the butter and cream but do not let them boil, then stir the mixture thoroughly into the potatoes with a large wooden spoon. Stir in the garlic then the cheese. Over a very low heat, with a heat-diffusing mat underneath the saucepan, stir the mixture until it is beautifully smooth and velvety. Take care that it doesn't turn grainy – don't let it get too hot. Serve immediately.

Jasmin Potato

This recipe is dedicated to Jasmin Amer, who was a good friend of my daughter Kate in junior school. Sometimes it can be hard work getting kids to eat cheese, and this simple dish solved all the problems – and the girls loved making it themselves. I thank not only the lovely sweet-natured Jasmin, but also her inventive mother.

- ◆ a good-sized baking potato
- ◆ butter or margarine
- ◆ salt
- ◆ plain cottage cheese, either low or medium fat
- ◆ grated farmhouse Cheddar, medium strength

Bake the jacket potato as usual. When it's ready, take it out and split it in half. Scoop out the flesh into a bowl, being careful not to break the skin. Stir in enough butter or margarine to make a nice creamy consistency and add salt to taste. In the bottom of the potato skins place a tablespoon or so of cottage cheese, pile in the potato mixture and put a good amount of grated Cheddar on top. Grill until the cheese melts and starts to toast. You can serve it with some crispy bacon, or stir some chopped chives into the cottage cheese, or, indeed, use a crumbly goat's cheese instead of the cottage cheese, but my kids have always liked it just as Jasmin's mother invented it.

PASTA

The Best Ever Pesto Sauce

- 150 g pine nuts, as fresh as possible
- 2 fat garlic cloves, new season's if possible, peeled
- 150 g Pecorino Foggiano, or Pecorino Romano, rind removed
- 100 g Pecorino Sardo DOC, the black-rinded strongest-flavoured one, rind removed
- 100 g Parmigiano Reggiano Staggionato, 3-year-old if possible, rind removed
- 80 g young Grana Padano, rind removed
- handful fresh basil leaves, finely chopped
- extra-virgin olive oil – choose a peppery Tuscan or fruity Puglian

First, toast the pine nuts, although if the nuts are *really* fresh and creamy-tasting you needn't bother: the result will be a creamier paste, which I prefer. You can tell how fresh they are by squeezing a kernel between your thumb and forefinger: it should 'burst' easily, then cream together between your fingers and should taste rich and nutty, without that cardboard stale flavour often found in the older ones. If you want to toast them, spread a layer on a baking tray and put them into the oven at 180°C/350°F/Gas Mark 4 until golden. If you're in a hurry, fry them. Cool them and mince them with the garlic.

Grate the Pecorino Foggiano or Romano, the Pecorino Sardo DOC, the Parmigiano, and the Grana Padano. Pound the basil with the nuts and garlic, and mix in the cheese. Taste, and add more basil or nuts to taste. Add a thin drizzle of olive oil to give a moist, dropping consistency. Remember, the better the ingredients, the better the taste.

This highly aromatic, fruity, gritty sauce clings tightly to pasta, and is the quickest pick-me-up after a night on the tiles.

A Simple Summer Meal

Steam some baby vegetables, such as asparagus, leeks, French beans and peas, then toss them into pasta coated with a tablespoon of pesto (or more if you like). Reckon on 250 g vegetables to 500 g dried pasta. Stir in a heaped tablespoon of rich *crème fraîche* or *fromage blanc* off the heat, carefully mixing it through the pasta and vegetables. Roughly chop around 2 tablespoons flat-leaf parsley, tough stalks removed, and chives, and turn them through the pasta. Grate over a young, moist Pecorino Toscano and serve. Enough for 2 as a main course or 4 as a starter.

Note: If you can't find baby vegetables just cut up larger ones into small chunks, but discard fibrous asparagus stalks, or the tougher parts of leeks, and use frozen peas as a substitute for fresh ones.

Cheese Wafers

Finding the right biscuits to accompany cheese is difficult since so many of the shop varieties have sugar added, which doesn't balance well with the sharp or fruity qualities of cheeses. I love Scottish oatcakes, the ones that are high baked and unsweetened, particularly Galloway's, which can be found in selected specialist cheese shops. The simple recipe below puts the pasta machine to another use, and makes enough to keep you going for a while, as they can be stored in an airtight container. But don't expect them to stay around for too long, as when anyone knows they're around it's a case of 'I've started, so I'll finish.'

- 430 g plain unbleached organic flour
- 2 tablespoons fine sea salt
- 1½ teaspoons ground white pepper
- 125 ml good olive oil, but not necessarily extra-virgin

- 15 g fresh yeast or the equivalent dried
- pure spring or filtered water to bind
- 1 egg, beaten

FOR THE TOPPING
- mixed herbs, or caraway seeds, or grated Parmesan, plus coarse sea salt (optional)

Make the mixture the evening before you want to eat the biscuits, as you need to leave the dough to rise overnight.

Either in a food-processor or by hand mix together the flour, salt and pepper. Drizzle in the oil and bind to a paste. Dissolve the yeast in a little warm water then add to the flour and mix to a dough.

Knead either by hand on a floured surface or with the bread hook of a food-processor, and make sure you blend the dough thoroughly with good strong hand movements, until it is smooth and holding together, 5 minutes or a little longer. Cover with a clean kitchen cloth and leave somewhere warm and without draughts for around 30 minutes. Then knead again on a floured surface for 10 minutes. Cover with clingfilm and place in the fridge overnight, or for at least 12 hours.

With your pasta machine on number 1, start rolling the dough through, turning up the notch after each roll until you finish at number 8 – the dough is passed through 8 times. It should be very thin. You can roll out by hand 8 times, but it may be easier to take small walnut-size pieces of dough, roll them into balls, place each individually on a lightly floured surface and roll out into a thin flat circle.

Preheat the oven to 200°C/400°F/Gas Mark 6.

Brush the rolled-out dough with the eggwash, sprinkle with coarse sea salt and herbs, seeds or Parmigiano Reggiano, if using, then cut it into triangles, squares or rounds. Put them on to a greased and floured baking sheet, or on baking parchment on a baking sheet, and slide it on to the middle shelf of the oven. Bake for around 7 minutes until golden. Cool on wire racks.

Pasta Jalfrezi

Haloumi cheese is often grilled on the barbecue or pan-fried and served with a mixed salad. However, my brother Douglas, who loves pasta, and his ever inventive wife, Shasna, came up with this interesting mix of flavours and textures. Shasna stressed that the spices must be really fresh – buy them from specialist shops, suppliers or markets: they lose their delicacy and the nuances in flavour if they have been standing around for a long time.

Serves 2
- 4 tablespoons well-flavoured extra-virgin olive oil, e.g. from Puglia
- 2 plump cloves garlic, crushed
- 75 g haloumi cheese, cubed
- 1 medium onion, peeled and sliced
- 2 fresh red chillies, chopped – seeded if you don't like it too hot
- 1 courgette, finely sliced then blanched and patted dry
- ½ teaspoon paprika, hot or mild (your choice)
- ½ teaspoon turmeric
- ½ teaspoon garam masala
- 1 teaspoon cumin powder
- 2 teaspoons coriander powder
- 230 g slow-roasted vine tomatoes, or canned peeled plum tomatoes
- 250 g cooked fresh pasta of your choice
- 1 tablespoon fresh coriander, chopped
- freshly ground black pepper

Warm the olive oil in a heavy frying pan. Add the crushed garlic and the haloumi and cook until golden brown. Add the onion, chillies and courgettes, and cook until they are translucent. Tip in the paprika, turmeric, garam masala, cumin and coriander and stir for 2 minutes to toast the spices with the other ingredients. Add the tomatoes and cook for 2 more minutes. Stir in the cooked pasta and toss gently to coat completely. Scatter over the fresh coriander, add a grinding of black pepper and serve.

My Mozzarella di Bufala and Tomato Salad ◆ *p. 95*

Slow-oven-roasted vine tomatoes in olive oil and basil ◆ *p. 95*

Scallops with Walnut Vinegar Glaze and Fresh Sheep's Milk Cheese and Walnut Salad ◆ *p. 98*

Cubed Beaufort cheese and *pancetta lardons* on green leaves with walnut oil dressing ◆ *p. 99*

Salad of summer leaves with Rocamadour cream dressing ◆ *p. 99*

The Best Ever Pesto Sauce   ◆   *p. 115*

Pasta with Truffle Cheese   ◆   *p. 119*

Valençay and Chocolate Walnut Brownies ◆ *p. 143*

Summer fruits and Fontainebleu cream with mint and
lemon thyme ◆ *pp. 34-5*

The mighty Parmigiano Reggiano
(from the producer/maturer Cavola di Toano 993)

Melting Raclette cheese

Devon Blue Cream with Damson Cheese Scones ◆ *pp. 146–7*

Preparing Tête de Moine on a Girolle machine, to create florets of shaved cheese

L'Écu goat's cheeses (our own recipe)

Blue cheeses (Bleu d'Auvergne in blue foil)

Cornish Yarg

A salad of chopped cucumber, finely sliced red onion, halved cherry tomatoes and mixed olives, all tossed in a fruity olive oil with a little salt and coarsely ground black pepper, makes a refreshing accompaniment.

Pasta with Truffle Cheese

The truffle auction each November in Alba, which is situated in the Piedmont region of northern Italy, is always exciting, as absurd amounts of money are bid for the strange-looking knobbly dark funghi, which have been snuffled out of the ground by dogs or pigs trained to recognize their distinct earthy aroma. Truffles are used freshly grated, or to aromatize oils and dried pasta, or made into pastes and fillings.

However, the most pleasurable way I have found to use them is with cheese. When I started my business in 1991 I searched out a truffle cheese from Piedmont which, although expensive, was not so absurdly priced that it was out of reach. While it can be used as a table cheese, I love to shave it over pasta or risotto for the luxurious taste and aroma.

- 500 g fine *tagliatelle*, either fresh or dried
- a little extra-virgin olive oil
- 125 g *fromage blanc* or *fromage frais*, low- or full-fat
- freshly ground black pepper
- a few sage leaves, finely chopped
- 250 g Formaggio di Tartufo, a hard cow and goat's milk cheese, or Caprini Tartufo, a fresh goat's milk cheese with shavings of truffle on top

Cook the pasta until it is *al dente*, then drain it well. Put it back into the pan, toss it in the olive oil to coat it lightly, then stir in the *fromage blanc* or *fromage frais*, some black pepper and the sage. Reheat it for a few moments. Pile the pasta on to a dish, or plate, then grate or crumble over the cheese. With two large forks gently lift the pasta so that the cheese can mingle loosely but not get lost. Serve immediately with a salad of mixed leaves, dressed with a little truffle oil and walnut vinegar – or a good-quality wine vinegar that's not overpowering.

A Travelling Tale

ITALIAN CHEESE AND A TRIP TO EMILIA ROMAGNA

The French have clear opinions on the superiority of their cheese, but it is little known how the Italians influenced and guided their neighbours in the art of cheesemaking.

I have made it a mission to search out and make contact with Italian suppliers and producers of traditional farmhouse cheeses, as it is rare to see their products other than in their immediate region. Importers tend to bring in the mass-produced and easily accessible goods that have a long storage date, rather than nurturing and promoting more particular varieties. And business is business – but I am a small fish, so to speak, so I can take a different stance. Take Parmigiano Reggiano, for instance. It is available everywhere, either in shrink-wrapped pieces, or ready-grated – very useful for coating pasta or shaving fashionably over salads. However, the taste can be underpowered and rather soapy. Why? Because the cheese is young – barely 24 months old – and not of the finest grade. Just like a pre-wrapped factory-made Cheddar alongside a farmhouse-made cloth-wrapped one, the taste is completely different. As far as I am concerned, and I have tasted many Parmigiano cheeses in my time, I prefer the 3-year-matured ones from Reggia Emilia, which is the original grazing zone, rather than from Parma or Modena. How do I know where the cheese comes from? The stamped numbers on the side of the crust denote the month and year the cheese was made, the Parmigiano Reggiano stamp showing it is made to the required standards of manufacture, and the number of the zone where the cheesemaker is based. The lower numbers (under 2000) denote Reggia Emilia, and the higher ones (2000 upwards) Parma and Modena.

I choose number 993 from Tavola di Toano, a producer of fine-flavoured cheese with a fruity rich flavour and creamy crumbliness. This is a cheese to savour as part of your cheeseboard or as an appetizer with champagne or spumante. Cheesemongers specializing in farmhouse cheeses will also do their best to obtain the finest quality Parmigiano, to give their customers the opportunity of enjoying the cheese in its own right rather than just as a culinary ingredient.

We tend to associate Italy with the Mediterranean – pasta with fresh tomatoes, pesto made with a mixture of Pecorino Romano, Foggiano, Toscana and nutty Parmigiano. With those colourful dishes from Tuscany and the south, using flakes of hard Pecorino or melted mozzarella, you're apt to think that in Italy cheese is always cooked. How wrong you can be. In fact, Italy should be divided into two different countries: north and south. The Milanese would prefer this as, hard-working and serious-minded, they feel they are propping up the more languid southerners who believe life is to be enjoyed at a snail's pace rather than in the rat race.

It is in the north that you find the most interesting and complex cheeses, and it is always an adventure for me to visit and taste cheese from the Piedmont area to Venezia, supplemented by the delicious wines of the region.

A professional and powerful consortium protects and safeguards cheeses under the DOC label, rather like the French AOC. If only they would devise a Guild of Specialist Cheesemakers for people like me to join, then Italian cheeses would be taken more seriously.

Many Italian alpine cheeses resemble French ones, and indeed have similar names. Reblechon, pronounced with the hard *ch* as in 'church', is much the same as the French Savoie cheese Reblochon, except that it is slightly smaller and ripens faster. The shape of a *toma* is similar to that of a *tomme* in France, and the textures are again supple, crumbly and aromatic, but the Italian versions have a floral, rounded taste, and some are coated with herbs, or in summer, rocket or sorrel leaves. We experiment with them in our maturing room to bring out the intensity of their flavour with the rich creamy texture.

Again in the Piedmont area the goat's cheeses are superb – lighter and milder than their French counterparts, yet with that direct acidic quality that goes so well with the fresh, dry Gaia wines. They are startling white, topped with shaved fresh black truffles. The earthy aroma coupled with the creamy, tangy taste is so enticing and beguiling.

Asiago is a versatile, noble cheese, rather like an Emmental, and can be put to a multitude of uses. A cheese of character, its milky, nutty taste and supple texture changes after careful handling in the maturing room over a year into the hard, fruity, crumbly Asiago Vezzena, a cheese of elegance and style, to be accompanied, perhaps, by a full, fruity Valpolicella.

And what about Gorgonzola? Dolcelatte is a mass-produced version. If you want a soft blue cheese go for Gorgonzola *dolce cremificato*. The hard blue cheese is Gorgonzola *naturale* (not mountain Gorgonzola). The *dolce* is velvety rich with a nutty bite and the pale blue vein seeping into the cheese. The harder cheese is densely veined and tastes full-bodied with a strident directness – perfect with walnuts and a fine old Barolo. The *torta*, with its layers of mascarpone and *dolce* cheeses, is rich and fruity-tasting, probably a bit overpowering during the summer.

One of the first cheeses I imported as a farmhouse-made variety was Taleggio. This washed-rind cheese, which originated in the Val Taleggio area in the Bergamo province, and which only acquired its name around the turn of the twentieth century, actually dates back to the tenth or eleventh century when cheese was made as a form of currency, rather like in France, and the method of making it was documented for the purpose of making its trade fair and equal. The Savoie region in France was part of Italy until the seventeenth century, which is why some of the cheeses are similar – Taleggio and Reblochon, Castelmagno and Bleu de Termignon, Fontina and Abondance. When you discover how important cheese is in Italy, not only as an ingredient for cooking, but as a staple, you begin to appreciate the home-made varieties as much as their French counterparts.

One of the best evenings I have ever spent in the guise of work was when I organized an Italian cheese dinner at the Groucho Club in Soho, with wine merchants Bibendum. It consisted of seven courses with wines to match. All of the dishes served included cheese – a tart, a soufflé, a ricotta and orange cake, a wild mushroom and truffle cheese lasagne – and it worked so well that awareness and interest were generated in both media and restaurants. That evening I met Rose Gray of the River Café in west London, and our association is still going strong eight years later.

Italy is more acutely aware of the importance of – and more forward-thinking than other European countries – maintaining the survival of its cheeses and the continuance of traditional methods of production, whether in small dairies or larger government-maintained factories. However, it is only when searching out the more rustic farmhouse varieties that the true tastes, textures and aromas are appreciated.

A TRIP TO EMILIA ROMAGNA IN LATE OCTOBER 1997

At this time of year I am getting myself into a lather about Christmas. Or, more precisely, about how I am going to tempt and seduce my customers with interesting produce. By way of diversion, in 1997 I took a stormblasting trip to Emilia Romagna, in Italy. I'd already organized all the produce from France, but Italy always comes up trumps in sweetmeats and festive fare. It might seem crazy to dash around like a mad fool for four days trying to pin down particular producers, but one of the reasons I started my business was to satisfy an urgent need for authentic artisanal goods seldom seen outside their own particular area. We may bow and scrape to the stellar chefs, who all seem to be men, don't they?, but to my mind it is we women who are cooks in the purest sense, and I, for one, want to use original ingredients – Italian-made ricotta, sausages and salami from Romagna, properly aged Parmigiano Reggiano. Nothing less will do.

We were busy in the shop and with restaurant work and I couldn't leave before the end of the day on Saturday. No matter: the underground from Arsenal whisked me to Heathrow direct in an hour and ten minutes, which gave me time to wind down and make notes for the trip. I took a late Alitalia flight, but the disgraceful tray of food presented on board made me reflect wistfully about what and where I'd rather be eating – a serious Scottish breakfast on the Isle of Eriska, or tea at an elegant café in Prague, or lunch at the tiny restaurant-gallery on the island of Valentia off the coast of Kerry, cocktails on a yacht moored off the Costa Smeralda in Sardinia, or a late-evening dinner at an intimate clubby restaurant in downtown Manhattan.

Touching down at Milan airport lifted my spirits, and I met up with my colleague and fellow foodie Geoff Owen. We talked for a few hours, plotting and planning the next few days.

Sunday morning arrived too soon, as I was woken at 6.30 a.m. with the pop-pop-popping of shotguns as the Italians partook of their favourite weekend sport, shooting anything small and furry, or small with fluttering wings. No wonder I seldom heard birdsong in the mornings, and have never known an Italian child keep a pet rabbit. But an early start was necessary, as we had to drive quite a way to Bologna where lunch was booked at a rustic *osteria* with a suitably nostalgic menu.

However, I could not leave Milan without breakfast at Gatullo, a *pasticceria* on the Piazzale di Porta Lodovica 2, in a chic residential area off the Via Italia. This is where the local gentry and soigné clientele ponder and test the patience of the staff before making their choice. There is a small area to the side of the shop where you can gulp down a heady espresso with a morning croissant, crisp on the outside and warm and flaky within. The real reason for coming here, though, was for the glacé chestnuts, made on the premises and simply the most delicious confection, not too sweet, retaining their bite and earthy, woody texture – always a success. If only I could have brought back the exotic chocolates and gorgeously opulent cakes and pastries too.

As we raced out of Milan on that pale autumn morning, the thin, shimmering sun reflected against the majestic sombre brickwork of the city buildings and the wide avenues of poplar trees that lined our route out of town and on to the motorway. We reached Bologna in good time, left our suitcases at the hotel then zoomed off for lunch. There was just enough time to stop for a pre-lunch stroll outside Castello di Serravale, where we witnessed a wedding crowd gathered in front of the local church eyeing up a gorgeous object – not the bride but the sleek, sexy lines of a buttercup-yellow Ferrari F40 waiting for the happy couple to roar off into the sunset.

At the Osteria di Rubiara di Pedroni Italo we had to negotiate the bulky frame of the owner waiting at the entrance like some bouncer at an invitation-only night at the Camden Palace. Had we booked? Yes, we replied hesitantly, my colleague giving his name, which he (Signor Pedroni) pronounced exaggeratedly as Signor O-r-w-e-n. Signor Italo was not enamoured of the English surname but reluctantly let us in. The restaurant was sparsely furnished, in a typical simple country style, and the kitchen was almost domestic in size and layout. The other tables were filled with local family groups of all ages. No menu today as it was Sunday, but we would be fed a homely repast of regional specialities. We would drink the local Lambrusco *secco* (rather than the sweet version available in Britain). This is a *frizzante* red wine (the fizz comes from bottling the wine quickly then letting it ferment), and rather refreshing, with the heavy, rich local food.

Antipasti was a light chicken broth with fingernail-sized *tortellini* filled with minced *prosciutto*, over which we dusted a young but fruity grated Parmigiano Reggiano. Then came local *garganelli* pasta (folded cut ribbons) with a Bolognese sauce, simple and tasty – just very finely minced veal and pork in a tomato and beef stock. Next was *arrosto misto* – roasted meats, such as rabbit in a dark sticky sauce, a slice of veal loin, pork ribs, guinea-fowl leg, with an accompaniment of local salad leaves, some bitter, others buttery, with fennel, slightly green tomatoes, celery, and a dressing of prize-winning balsamic vinegar from Signor Italo's cellar – and I duly made a note to order the range for the shop – and Puglian olive oil. We had just enough room for the plate of small sponge cakes, almond, chocolate, chocolate and almond, and hazelnut meringue, with tastings of five different *grappe* made on the premises: nut, which tasted like syrup of figs, raspberry, orange, blackberry and plain. A good *grappa* has delicacy and finesse before the fire hits the throat, and all of these were of a high quality. All I wanted after that was a strong espresso, and a walk in the fresh air to bring me back to my senses.

We spent the rest of that afternoon visiting the hillside abbey at Monteveggio where a silent order of monks live alongside a silent order of nuns. Only in Italy . . . However, the parkland walks are reviving, with lovely open views.

I won't bore you with all the blind alleys and lost causes I endured on this trip, but what I did find was the perfect fresh pasta from Celestino. It was simply heaven on a plate. The tasting took place in the side office beside the production line, as I tried to explain I wanted most of the fillings to be vegetarian. Blank looks made me wonder what the hell I was doing in Emilia Romagna, home of the pig and all its parts. It took all my charm and persuasive intent to get through to them.

The other great find was a real meaty mortadella with truffles from Signor Bidinelli, whose hands showed his years of labour. His left index finger was missing and his right middle fingertip too. However, his produce was among the best I'd ever seen – *zampone*, *cotechino*, fresh sausages, salami and hams of beautiful colour and texture. It's at times like these that I wish *bollito misto* would appear in every food writer's column, and trendy restaurants would remember the tradition of boiled meats and vegetables in broth. Fuel food for winter warmth, but also encapsulating the seasonal ingredients.

Before returning to London, I spent an early morning at Milan fruit and vegetable market where I met Signor Pirola and his son Alessandro, who bring their dewy fresh salad leaves, herbs and leafy vegetables from their farm just outside the city. Then I had time for a quick visit to a cheese supplier where I chose some rather interesting Pecorinos, fresh and crumbly, as well as ricotta made with sheep and cow's milk, and fresh goat's milk cheeses.

All in all it was a successful trip – and my family enjoyed the *bollito misto* on my return.

PASTRY, TARTS AND DESSERTS

Panzerotti

A typical Neapolitan-style sweet pastry, to accompany a strong espresso or a liqueur, like the famous orange-yellow Strega from Benevento made with herbs and spices.

FOR THE PASTRY
- 250 g unbleached organic plain flour
- 50 g unsalted butter
- 50 g caster sugar
- 1 free-range organic egg
- a little milk
- sunflower or groundnut oil for deep frying
- icing sugar

FOR THE FILLING
- 500 g very fresh ricotta (cow or buffalo milk or fresh Sairass)
- 2 tablespoons mascarpone
- 100 g vanilla-scented caster sugar
- 1 free-range organic egg yolk
- grated rind of 1 lemon and 1 orange, blanched for two minutes then drained and dried on paper towel

To make the pastry by hand, sieve the flour into a bowl and drop in the cold butter in tiny pieces. Rub together until the mixture resembles fine crumbs then mix in the sugar. Knead in the egg until the texture is smooth, adding a little milk to make it pliable but not sticky. Take it out of the bowl and place it on a lightly floured surface. Continue to knead for at least 10 minutes until the dough is elastic. Cover and let it rest in the fridge for 30 minutes or so.

To make the pastry in a food-processor, sieve the flour into a bowl and drop in the cold butter in small pieces. Pulse at a low speed, 'staccato', until the mixture resembles fine crumbs. Add the sugar, and pulse in the egg until the dough is smooth. Take it out of the bowl and place it on a lightly floured surface. Knead for at least 5 minutes, adding a little milk to make the dough pliable and elastic. Leave to rest as above.

Mix the filling ingredients together in a bowl. Take the pastry out of the fridge and roll it out thinly, then cut out approximately 50 7.5 cm rounds. Put a tablespoon of filling in the middle of each round, then brush the edges of the pastry with a little milk before placing another round on top. Pinch the edges to seal and crimp them.

Deep-fry the pastry pillows a few at a time, turning them gently to cook evenly – you want to achieve a golden pastry. As they start to turn golden whip them out of the oil and shake off the excess before placing them on paper towels to drain thoroughly. Serve warm, dusted with icing sugar.

Caramelized Shallots with Fourme d'Ambert on Flaky Pastry

This tatin makes an impressive first course, or special lunchtime treat. You can buy really good-quality ready-made flaky pastry from supermarkets; or order it from a decent *pâtisserie* or bakery.

- 250 g frozen or fresh flaky pastry
- 200 g unsalted butter
- 500 g shallots, walnut-sized, peeled
- 250 g Fourme d'Ambert, or a creamy blue cheese that's not too aggressive in flavour
- 115 g *fromage blanc* or *fromage frais*, low or full fat
- 125 ml double cream (optional)
- sea salt and freshly ground black pepper to taste
- 1 tablespoon fresh thyme leaves, finely chopped

Preheat the oven to 200°C/400°F/Gas Mark 6.

Roll out the pastry in a 20-cm circle and lightly score around the edge, about 2.5 cm in, with the tip of a cook's knife; this will help lift the edges when cooking. Place it on a lightly oiled baking sheet. (Alternatively you can use it to line a shallow tart tin.) Prick over the base and brush it with beaten egg white, which helps to keep the pastry crisp.

In a heavy frying-pan melt the butter until it is foamy then put in the shallots and cook until they become golden brown and caramelized (a teaspoon or two of balsamic vinegar adds an extra sweet-and-sour zesty taste). Take off the heat and scoop the shallots into a bowl to cool to room temperature. Reduce any liquid in the pan to a thick caramelized syrup and add it to the shallots.

In another bowl mash the cheese with the *fromage blanc* or *fromage frais* and the cream, if using. Add salt and pepper to taste, and fold in the thyme.

Spread the cheese mixture over the pastry to where you've scored the edge, then place the shallots on top. Bake on the middle shelf until the pastry is golden and the filling nicely cooked.

Serve warm rather than hot, with a light fruity wine.

Caramelized Apples with Lancashire Cheese on Flaky Pastry

Here is a lovely warming recipe for late autumn. If you can get hold of really good apples, such as the Kent variety from Brogdale Horticultural Trust, or whatever might be available at your local Farmers' Market, all the better.

- 250 g frozen or fresh flaky pastry
- 200 g unsalted butter
- 3–4 large dessert apples, peeled, cored and sliced, not too thinly or they will disintegrate
- a little ground cinnamon or mixed spice
- thin slice quince cheese – fruit paste (optional)
- 2 teaspoons Demerara or fine Muscovado sugar
- 200 g Kirkham's or Shorrocks Lancashire, on the young side
- 120 g *fromage blanc* or *fromage frais*, low or full fat

Preheat the oven to 200°C/400°F/Gas Mark 6.

Roll out the pastry in a 20-cm circle, then score the edge, around 2.5 cm in, with the tip of a cook's knife. Place it on a lightly oiled baking sheet. (Alternatively, you can use it to line a shallow tart tin.) In a heavy frying-pan melt the butter until it is foamy then fry the apples until they are golden but still firm enough, not collapsing. Add the spice and quince cheese, if using, and sprinkle over the sugar, then continue cooking until everything is nicely caramelized. Take the pan off the heat and let the apples cool to room temperature. Reduce any juices in the pan to a thick syrup, then add it to the apples.

In a bowl crumble the cheese and mix in the *fromage blanc* or *fromage frais* until it is smooth but retains some texture. Spread over the pastry, lay the apples and their thickened juices on top, and bake on the middle shelf until the pastry is golden and the filling evenly cooked. Serve warm.

Apple or Cheese Strudel

I used to watch my grandpa prepare food on a smallish square kitchen table in the middle of his kitchen. It was a simple pine table fashionably faded from being scrubbed constantly and kept scrupulously clean. I asked him why he always used that table to prepare food, and he said it was because it was just the right height for all the laborious chores and that every good cook should have a table just like it. I'm not sure if trendy kitchen designers make strudel tables, but perhaps they should.

If you've mastered pasta-making, played around with breadmaking, and given the fresh cheesemaking a shot, what better way of showing off your dexterity than making your own strudel pastry to wrap round your fresh cheese?

Priorities
- Have a free weekend
- Turn off the phone and computer
- Put a sign on the door for callers to knock gently
- Have enough space in the kitchen to work: you need to be able to walk around the table as you stretch the dough

- Play your favourite music softly in the background
- The room should be warm and without a through draught
- Don't be in a hurry: relax and smile

Serves at least 18

FOR THE PASTRY
- 200 g high-gluten plain flour
- 1 large free-range organic egg
- 2 level teaspoons caster sugar
- 1.5 tablespoons organic groundnut or sunflower oil, cold-pressed, if possible
- approximately 150 ml spring water, warmed
- icing sugar

FOR THE APPLE FILLING
- 1.5 kg cooking apples, or hard, tart eating apples such as Katy or Kent
- 120 g dry breadcrumbs – white bread rubbed into crumbs, dried out in the oven, then crushed
- 170–220 g caster sugar, according to how tart the apples are
- 170 g unsalted butter, melted, or sunflower oil

FOR THE CREAM CHEESE FILLING
- 120 g fine breadcrumbs
- 50 g butter, melted
- 650 g fresh cream cheese
- 2 medium organic eggs, separated
- 120 g unsalted butter
- 120 g fine vanilla caster sugar
- zest of 1 lemon, blanched and dried
- juice of 1 lemon
- 30 g Lexia raisins or sultanas, soaked in a little sweet wine for 1 hour then drained
- 2 tablespoons ground almonds
- melted butter or oil and sugar

On your clean work surface, place the sieved flour in a mound and make a well in the centre. Pour in the egg, sugar and oil and with a knife 'cut' into the flour, drawing it into the centre to mix it into a crumbly mass. Add a little water, to make a sticky but not too wet blob, rather like a scone mixture. Then, with the palm of your hand, knead the dough, drawing the pastry towards and away from you in free movements to make a velvety-smooth texture. Humming helps. Then place it on a clean board and put a pudding basin over it like a helmet. Rest the dough for around 30 minutes while you make the filling.

For the apple filling, peel, core and slice the apples, then place them in a bowl of acidulated water (water to which lemon juice has been added). Have ready the other ingredients.

For the cheese filling, mix the breadcrumbs with the melted butter and lay them on a baking sheet in the oven to dry out at 200°C/400°F/Gas Mark 6. When they have turned pale gold, take them out and crush them to fine grains. Put the cream cheese into a bowl and beat in the egg yolks until smooth. Cream 120 g butter with the sugar. Fold the cheese mixture into the creamed butter. Stir in the lemon zest, juice and raisins. Whisk the egg white to stiff peaks and fold into the cheese mixture.

Preheat the oven to 200°C/400°F/Gas Mark 6.

To stretch the dough: cover the table with a clean cloth, making sure the end nearest to you hangs over the edge. Rub a little sieved flour over the cloth. Place the dough in the middle and gently roll it out in a circle around 30 cm diameter or a little more. Brush it with oil or melted butter, then lightly dust your hands with flour, shaking off any excess. Now, with the back of your hands uppermost, wiggle your hands under the dough circle and gently pull the dough back with your knuckles, making the circle a little larger. Walk round the table easing out the dough in this way, stretching and pulling gently. If it splits, press it together to mend it. It's ready when you have paper-thin pastry. Just trim off any thick bits around the edges and shape it into a rectangle.

To fill and roll it with apple: sprinkle the half of the pastry nearest to you with the breadcrumbs. Take the apple slices out of the acidulated water and pat them dry on paper towels. Lay them evenly over the breadcrumbs, cover them with sugar and almost all of the butter or oil. Brush the other end of the pastry with the rest of the butter or oil and sprinkle with sugar. Now, gently but purposefully, start to roll: lift up the cloth in both hands and ease it over, like a swiss roll, until you get to the end. Secure the ends of your long sausage by pressing down, then place the strudel as carefully as possible on a lightly oiled and floured baking sheet. Make the sausage into a crescent to get it on to the tray. Brush over the remaining butter or oil and bake for 30 minutes, turning down the heat to 190°C/375°F/Gas Mark 5 after 15 minutes if it starts to brown too quickly. Serve warm, dusted with icing-sugar and accompanied with *crème fraîche*.

To fill and roll it with cheese: scatter the breadcrumbs and the ground almonds over the pastry dough, as above, then spread the cheese filling over the half of the pastry nearest to you. Spread the other half with melted butter or oil and sugar, roll up and bake as above. Serve dusted with icing sugar. Strong coffee is an ideal accompaniment.

Fruit Confit with Spiced Syrup

The warm spice notes mingling with the fruits are very Christmassy, and I think this would be lovely with Crème Chantilly (see page 35) or served alongside the richly dark Torte Cioccolate (see page 140).

- 1 litre spring water
- 1 kg caster sugar
- 4 cloves
- 2 sticks cinnamon
- 1 vanilla pod
- 3 star anise
- a few crushed mustard seeds
- 2 oranges
- 2 clementines
- 1 pink grapefruit
- 1 pineapple
- 1–2 star fruits (optional)
- granulated sugar

In a heavy-bottomed stainless-steel saucepan bring the water to the boil with the caster sugar, then put in the cloves, cinnamon, vanilla, star anise and mustard seeds. Cook over a medium heat for 5–10 minutes while you prepare the fruit. Peel the pineapple but leave the skins on the rest of the fruit. Cut the oranges, clementines and grapefruit into eighths, the pineapple into chunks, the star fruit (if using) into its natural star shape. Put the fruit into the syrup and simmer gently for 1½–2 hours or until it is translucent. Take out the fruit, lay it on a grill pan lined with foil, shake over the granulated sugar and grill until golden and starting to brown. Reduce the syrup and drizzle it over the fruit before serving.

Pain Perdu

'Lost Bread' is a simple dish often ruined by awful bread, or a heavy hand with the butter it's fried in. You can add some cinnamon to the vanilla sugar to give a spicier flavour, or substitute a fruit and nut bread for the brioche, but make sure the bread is of the best quality as this is crucial to the flavour.

- 5 medium eggs
- 125 g caster sugar
- seeds of 1 vanilla pod
- 500 ml full fat milk
- 6 slices from a large brioche loaf or 3 brioche buns, halved
- 250 g clarified butter (see Note)

Mix the eggs with the sugar and vanilla seeds. Add the milk and blend thoroughly. Put the mixture into a large dish. Lay the bread in it and coat it well with the milk mixture. Cover the dish and leave it in the fridge for 3 hours. Take it out and shake off the residue of the milk mixture, then fry the soaked bread in the clarified butter. Serve warm with raspberries tossed in Maraschino liqueur and a little caster sugar, or with the Fruit Confit (see page 135), and Crème Chantilly (see page 35) or Sheep's Milk Ice-cream (page 158).

Note: To clarify butter, melt the butter in a double saucepan – the top pan should not touch the simmering water in the lower one. Line a fine sieve with double muslin, which you have dipped in warm water then squeezed well, and set it over a bowl. Pour the butter into the sieve and let it drip into the bowl. A thick residue will be left in the muslin and the clear butterfat in the bowl, ready for use.

Leek and Goat's Cheese Tart with Fromage Blanc

The addition of *fromage blanc* to the egg-free cream filling gives a lighter texture.

FOR THE PASTRY
- 200 g unbleached organic plain flour, sieved
- pinch of fine sea salt
- 150 g unsalted chilled butter, cut into small pieces
- 1 organic egg yolk, mixed with 2 tablespoons iced spring water

FOR THE FILLING
- 100 g unsalted Charente butter
- 3 large leeks, trimmed, washed and finely sliced
- finely chopped thyme and oregano
- fine sea salt and freshly ground black pepper
- 300–400 ml *fromage blanc*, 40 per cent fat
- 250 ml organic single cream or rich creamy milk
- 150–180 g Sainte-Maure goat's cheese, or similar goat's cheese log, sliced young soft Brie de Chèvre or Brie de Meaux, the crust removed if hard or a milder taste is preferred, or a mixture of your choice

Preheat the oven to 200°C/400°F/Gas Mark 6.

Put the flour into a bowl then add the salt and rub in the chilled butter until the mixture resembles fine breadcrumbs. Add the water and egg mixture, and mix until the texture is smooth. Or you can make the pastry in the food-processor.

Rest the pastry if it was made by hand, or you can use it immediately if you made it in the food-processor. Take a 30-cm tart tin, lightly butter and flour it, then shake out the excess flour. Line the tin with the pastry. Prick the base. Place greaseproof paper over it and fill it with baking beans. Bake blind for around 10 minutes. Remove the paper and baking beans and pop the tin back into the oven for another 5 minutes to colour the pastry slightly. Cool the pastry a little before putting in the filling.

In a large frying-pan melt the butter and sweat the leeks until they are soft and lightly golden. Add the herbs and a little salt and black pepper. In a bowl mix the *fromage blanc* with the cream, then stir in the leeks, drained of any excess liquid. Pour the mixture into the tart tin and smooth it to the edges. Slice the cheese over the top and place the tin on a baking sheet before sliding it into the oven on the middle shelf for around 15–20 minutes. Check from time to time to see that the cheese is melting nicely but not over-browning. Take it out when the top is pale gold coloured and the filling is set.

Tarte au Fromage Blanc

If you have gone to the trouble of making your own *fromage blanc*, use it in this tart! When you cut into the tart's mahogany-coloured crust to release the fluffy white filling, you will find you have one of the best classic sweet cheese desserts. Turn it upside down soon after it has been removed from the oven, otherwise it sinks and looks less spectacular. It goes perfectly with Pacherenc de Vendemiaire, the 'smoky' sweet version of Pacherenc du Vic Bihl, from Alain Brumont's estate in Maumusson, Gers, in south-west France.

FOR THE RICH SHORTCRUST PASTRY
- 500 g unbleached organic flour
- a good pinch of fine sea salt
- 250 g best-quality chilled unsalted butter, cut into tiny cubes
- around 50 g sieved icing sugar
- 2 egg yolks, mixed with 5 tablespoons iced spring water

- 500 ml full-fat milk
- 1 vanilla pod, split
- 5 large free-range organic eggs, as fresh as possible
- zest of 1 lemon, blanched, drained and dried
- 125 g caster sugar
- 80 g ground rice
- 400 g well-drained 40 per cent fat *fromage blanc*
- 100 g mascarpone
- 1 egg, beaten, to glaze
- icing sugar

Preheat the oven to 200°C/400°F/Gas Mark 6.

Sieve the flour and salt into the food-processor bowl, drop in the butter and pulse until it resembles breadcrumbs. Add the sugar, buzz briefly, then with the motor running, pour in the egg and water in a steady stream until the dough forms a ball that is not too wet – it should not be too sticky. You may not need to use all of the egg and water. Or make the pastry by hand in the usual way. Let the dough rest for 30 minutes if it's hand-made, otherwise you can use it straight away.

Grease and flour a 25–30-cm loose-bottomed tart tin. Roll out the pastry and use it to line the tin, then prick the base. Put in a piece of greaseproof paper and fill it with baking beans. Bake for 10 minutes, then remove the paper and beans, and slide the tin back into the oven for a few more minutes to dry the base. You can use this right away or keep it until you want to fill it later in the day.

Preheat the oven to 200°C/400°F/Gas Mark 6.

Make the filling. Pour the milk into a saucepan, then scrape in the seeds from the vanilla pod, and drop in the pod. Bring it to the boil. Take it off the heat and cool completely.

Separate the eggs and put the whites into a very clean glass bowl that you have rubbed with half a lemon. Beat the sugar into the egg yolks until it becomes a pale smooth cream, and the sugar has dissolved. Remove the vanilla pod from the milk and slowly stir it into the egg yolk and sugar mixture with the ground rice. Put the bowl over a saucepan of simmering water, making sure that it doesn't touch the water, and stir continuously until it thickens to a custard. Take it off the heat. Mix the lemon zest into the *fromage blanc* and *mascarpone*, then fold the cheese into the custard. Whisk the egg whites until they form stiff peaks and fold them into the custard mixture. Pour into the cooled tart base and brush the top with beaten egg. This is a little fiddly – try dabbing it on. Put the tart into the oven on the middle shelf for 20–30 minutes, until it has a lovely golden brown top. Remove it from the oven and, as soon as you can safely handle the tin, turn it out, upside down, on to a cake rack and let it get cold. Turn it carefully the right way up (you may need to ease it with a flat, spatula-type knife) and sprinkle it generously with icing sugar.

Torte Cioccolate

As with the Panzerotti and Torta di Ricotta, I have to thank the lovely Salvatore and Anna who made many delectable products for my shop before, sadly, they moved back to Italy. Anna's lightness of touch with pastry came, I think, from the depths of her heart – she is such a beautiful person both in looks and demeanour. Her husband Salvatore was a tremendous character and his sons were gifted players in the Junior League at Arsenal Football Club. Arsenal's loss is Lazio's gain. Trying to extract a recipe from them was difficult, since the recipes were family heirlooms, so to speak.

- 6 large organic free-range eggs, separated
- 150 g self-raising flour
- 4 tablespoons Valrhona cocoa powder, or similar high density cocoa powder
- 200 g vanilla caster sugar, divided into 6 portions
- 4 tablespoons boiled water with 25 g unsalted butter melted into it – keep warm but not hot

- 2 kg mascarpone cheese
- 300 g caster sugar
- 200 g finest quality 70 per cent chocolate, preferably Valrhona, melted in a double boiler and cooled to lukewarm
- 3 large organic egg yolks or 125 g unsalted Charente butter, softened, or similar light-tasting butter
- Strega, Maraschino or brandy
- chocolate shavings or curls, to top the cake

Preheat the oven to 200°C/400°F/Gas Mark 6 and place a baking tray on the middle shelf for the tins to sit on. Generously grease 2 15-cm round springform cake tins with butter and flour, shaking off the excess flour. Place a circle of greased baking parchment at the bottom of each tin. Set aside.

Whisk the egg whites until they are stiff. Sift the flour and cocoa together into a bowl. Using either a wooden spoon, a balloon whisk or an electric whisk on medium speed, beat the egg yolks one at a time with 1 portion of the vanilla sugar into the whisked egg white until the mixture is thick, then add another egg yolk and a portion of sugar, until all the eggs and sugar have been used and the mixture is thick and holds its shape like a mousse. Carefully fold in, with a spatula, the flour and cocoa until it is fully amalgamated. Slowly pour in the hot water and melted butter, and with a metal spoon fold into the cake mixture, taking care to not beat hard. Pour the mixture into the two cake tins and smooth the top to level it. Place the tins on the baking sheet in the oven and bake for 25 minutes or until the cake feels firm but spongy. Watch out when baking anything with chocolate as it does tend to burn.

For the filling, mix the mascarpone with the sugar and chocolate, and stir in the beaten egg yolks which must be as fresh as possible. If you are not entirely confident about using raw eggs leave them out, and instead use the butter. However, either the eggs or the butter must be used as they give the mixture a certain density of flavour, and lustre.

Split the sponges in half to give you 4 rounds. Sprinkle over some of the Strega, Maraschino or brandy, and let it soak in. Don't be tempted to use too much – you don't want the sponge to fall apart. Sandwich the layers with a thick slick of mascarpone chocolate cream. Cover the top sponge with any cream you have left and shave long curls of chocolate over the top. Keep the cake cool and eat it at one sitting.

Torta di Ricotta

Another of Anna and Salvatore's cakes, which is especially good as a light dessert. If you can locate buffalo milk ricotta or a sheep's milk ricotta, the texture and consistency will be more interesting and lingering.

- 700 g ricotta, either cow's, sheep's or buffalo's milk
- 100 g very fresh soft goat's or sheep's milk cheese, without visible rind or with rind removed
- 200 g caster sugar
- grated zest of 1 orange and 1 lemon
- 1 vanilla pod, split
- 1 sponge cake (see pages 140–41): substitute the same quantity of flour for the cocoa powder, and 1 tablespoon lemon zest for the vanilla extract
- Strega, or another sweet liqueur
- icing sugar

Sieve the ricotta and the other cheese and mix it with the sugar and the lemon and orange zest. Scrape the seeds out of the vanilla pod and stir them in. Split the sponge cake and lace both pieces with the liqueur. Use the ricotta cream to sandwich together the sponge discs. Dust the top with a thick carpet of icing sugar. Serve with an orange salad, or on its own with coffee and liqueurs.

Cream Cheese, Honey and Pistachio Tart

A visit to the Middle East gave me the opportunity to taste some of my favourite ingredients, such as warm spices, like cinnamon, with almonds, and rich lamb casseroles sweetened with prunes and preserved lemons. A day spent getting lost in the maze of winding streets in old Jerusalem, exploring all the different cultural food markets, prompted this recipe. The sticky sweetness of the pastries, with the incredibly strong coffee, dazzles the senses into a sort of euphoric submission, and it is easy to see why it is called the land of milk and honey: the food has a soothing, comforting quality.

Blind bake a 25–30-cm sweet pastry shell (see Tarte au Fromage Blanc, page 138) for about 10 minutes, and let it cool slightly. Spread a thick layer of runny honey – chestnut (dark) or multi-flower (lighter) – across the base, then sprinkle over plenty of unsalted skinned and chopped pistachios. Whip up some *creamy* rich fresh cheeses, such as fresh light goat's cheese, a very young Explorateur, or Finn, or Brillat Savarin, with equal amounts of *fromage blanc* and mascarpone – I suggest 200 g cheese, 100 g *fromage blanc*, 100 g mascarpone, beaten together with 2 egg yolks – to a thick and mousse-like consistency, stir in vanilla-scented sugar to taste and a few drops of orange flower water. Bake at 200°C/400°F/Gas Mark 6 for 15–20 minutes. Cool, then spread over the top a densely packed layer of caster sugar and flash under the grill, or use a kitchen blow-torch, to caramelize the top.

Valençay and Chocolate Walnut Brownies

It doesn't happen very often, thank goodness, but when a delivery from France arrives with a box of beautifully fresh Valençay goat's milk cheeses that has been crushed, my heart sinks. What a waste, is the first thought, but then I hand them over to our ever-accommodating Klaus, who makes savoury goat's milk quiches for the shop. The last time it happened, though, Eric, our intrepid man with the golden hands, hurtled into my office exclaiming, rather like Archimedes, 'I've just sandwiched some of the Valençay with the Valrhona bittersweet chocolate and it's absolutely marvellous. It's a real discovery!' When I tasted it I couldn't believe quite how good it was. Then the grey matter took over and I made brownies with all the broken-up fresh cheeses. Here's the result.

- 125 g 70 per cent bittersweet dark Valrhona chocolate or similar, plus 50 g Valrhona cocoa powder or similar
- 200 g unsalted Charente butter, or other extra-fine butter, at room temperature
- 1 vanilla pod, split
- 3 large organic eggs, the freshest possible
- 400 g caster sugar
- 285 g unbleached organic plain white flour
- 1 heaped teaspoon bicarbonate of soda
- pinch of extra-fine organic salt – optional, if the cheese is salty
- 125 g lightly toasted walnuts, roughly broken
- 250 g very fresh light-tasting crumbly goat's cheese – it can be ash-coated like Valençay, but not too moist
- 100 g extra thick Greek yoghurt, or 20 per cent or 40 per cent fat *fromage blanc*
- 50 g semi-sweet dark chocolate, chopped into rough shards
- 100 g icing sugar, sieved

Preheat the oven to 180°C/350°F/Gas Mark 4. Grease and flour a 35 cm × 30 cm rectangular tin. In a double boiler, melt the 125 g chocolate with the cocoa and butter, stirring until it has melted, then set it aside to cool.

Scrape the vanilla seeds into a bowl, add the eggs and beat until light and foamy. Put in the caster sugar and beat into a pale, thick cream.

Sift together the flour, bicarbonate of soda and salt, then gradually add it to the egg mixture, stirring until it is well blended. Carefully incorporate the chocolate mixture and most of the walnuts.

Blend the cheese with the yoghurt or *fromage blanc*, the chocolate shards and icing sugar until it is creamy but still with lumpy bits. Stir in the remaining walnuts. Fold the cheese mixture into the chocolate mixture, just until it looks streaky and marbled. Pour it into the tin, and put it into the centre of the oven. Bake for 30–35 minutes, or until the cake feels set but not too firm to the touch.

Remove it from the oven and let it cool a little in the tin. Then turn it out on to a wire rack to cool completely before cutting it into cubes and dusting with icing sugar.

Muffins with Smoked Cheese and Corn Kernels

Quick and easy, with the minimum of mixing for a light, crumbly taste. Instead of smoked cheese try Cheddar, or buffalo mozzarella (add the liquid whey for a tangy taste), or goat's cheeses, either soft fresh or grated hard cheeses. With the Cheddar include sun-dried tomatoes. The goat's cheeses go well with chopped thyme and *pancetta*, in small dice, fried until golden and dried of excess fat on paper towels. For sweet muffins, try a very fresh light-textured goat's cheese with 4 tablespoons of caster sugar and a handful of sweet blueberries.

- 250 g plain white organic flour
- 125 g polenta with husk included
- 4 teaspoons baking powder
- 1 level teaspoon fine organic sea salt
- about 100 g cooked and cooled corn kernels, or tinned, but drained of any liquid
- about 150 g grated smoked Ashdown Foresters organic cheese or smoked Cheddar – or try buffalo mozzarella or your own favourite, plus 100 g for topping
- 2 medium organic free-range eggs
- 200 ml milk, or the whey from buffalo mozzarella, or a mixture of both
- 30 g unsalted butter, melted, or 65 ml sunflower oil

Preheat the oven to 200°C/400°F/Gas Mark 6. Line a 12-segment bun tin with paper cases.

In a mixing bowl combine all the dry ingredients with a few deft swirls. Make a well in the centre. Mix together the corn kernels, cheese and all the wet ingredients in a glass jug – don't overbeat, just loosely incorporate them – and pour it into the well, mixing quickly and lightly to a lumpy, floppy batter. If the mixture doesn't drop easily add a little more liquid. Don't overmix – this mixture needs little elbow grease. Plop a heaped dessertspoonful into each paper case, top with the rest of the grated cheese and bake on the middle shelf for about 20 minutes or until well risen and golden. Serve warm.

Devon Blue Cream with Damson Cheese

Devon Blue cheese comes from Totnes, a bustling market town whose fortunes have ebbed and flowed over the years. However, its architecture and location make it a romantic sightseeing destination, and a must for hunters of antique pine furniture and blue and white pottery. The narrow high street climbs up a steep hill towards the church – if I were a writer of detective fiction, in the style of, say, Agatha Christie, I'd like to set a story here. But I digress. Just off the high street you will see a small shop called Ticklemore Cheeses, with a quaint frontage and lovely aromas emanating from it every time the door is opened.

Robin Congdon produces blue cheeses in a continental style, a lovely nutty hard goat's cheese and small fresh goat's cheeses. The blue cheeses are made with a rich, buttery cow's milk, a tangy sheep's milk, and a pungent goat's milk. It is the cow's milk version, Devon Blue, that I invariably mix into a blue-cheese butter or cream.

This is a lovely way to serve an unusual 'cream tea'. The season for damsons is short and if the early summer has been quite severe the yield may be low. However, if you can get hold of a kilo or two around the middle to end of August, place them, whole, in a stone or earthenware container with an ovenproof lid and bake them very slowly until they are soft – if you wish, add a stick or two of cinnamon. Take them out of the oven, turn them into a saucepan and boil, not too rapidly, until the consistency is denser, less liquid. The stones should be visible at the top and easy to remove. Pass the fruit through a fine sieve and add 500 g sugar for every 2 kg of fruit (if you have vanilla sugar all the better), and simmer for about 30 minutes until the paste begins to candy or crystallize around the edges. Don't discard the stones: boil them in water, crack them open and add the kernels to the damson cheese for their flavour. Put the damson cheese into sterilized jars without lids, or earthenware bowls, and dry out in a barely warm oven. When set, place waxed paper over the paste to preserve it and keep it covered, or screw on lids before storing in a cool place. Fruit cheese is delicious sliced thinly and served with tangy hard cheeses, or fresh sheep's and goat's milk cheeses, as well as smoked or air-dried ham.

For the Devon Blue cream, mash 300 g cheese, not too smoothly, then add 125 g clotted cream and 100 g roughly chopped roasted almonds.

Make some scones, and split them when they are still slightly warm. Place a small mound of cheese on one half and a sliver of damson cheese on the other. Sandwich together and enjoy with a glass of not too sweet dessert wine or maybe a glass of Madeira.

Scones

Makes 8–10
- 225 g self-raising flour
- large pinch fine sea salt
- 25 g caster sugar (optional)
- 50 g unsalted butter in tiny cubes
- 150 ml plus 2 tablespoons full-fat milk
- 1 large organic free-range egg, beaten

Preheat the oven to 230°C/450°F/Gas Mark 8. Put in a non-stick baking sheet to warm. Sift the flour and salt together into a bowl. Stir in the sugar (if using), and rub in the butter until the mixture resembles fine breadcrumbs. Make a well in the centre and trickle in the milk, stirring until you have a soft sticky dough.

Drop the dough on to a well-floured surface, and knead lightly until it is smooth without cracks. Sift over a little flour, then roll it out with a floured rolling-pin 2 cm thick. Lightly flour a pastry-cutter or the rim of a wine-glass, and punch out circles. Don't twist the cutter as this will damage the dough. Re-roll it until you have punched out 8–10 scones. Or cut out the dough into triangles with a sharp knife. Pop them on to the warmed baking sheet, brush the tops with the beaten egg, and bake one shelf above the centre for around 8–10 minutes, or until they are nicely risen and golden. Cool on a wire rack, but remember that scones are best served warm. And please don't freeze or keep them for another day – they really are best eaten fresh.

Goat's Cheese Cheesecake with Prunes Soaked in Mahagastotte Champagne Tea

I love really good teas, and if you are a serious tea drinker, tea is not so simple to make as good tea needs to have time to brew. I prefer mine without milk unless I am dunking a teabag in a mug. It's a shame to spoil a delicate flavour with the intrusion of milk but that doesn't mean you can't eat something creamy with it! And in the piquant Mahagastotte tea from Nuwara Eliya in the Uva district of Sri Lanka, which Robert Wilson supplies to us, you have the perfect combination of taste and elegance. Soaking Agen prunes in this tea doesn't detract from their flavour either and served alongside this slightly sharp and sweet cheesecake you have a perfect dessert to savour, with tinkling teacups brimming with refreshing champagne tea rather than the ubiquitous shot of espresso.

I have given two recipes for the cheesecake filling, one cooked, the other not. The base recipe is the same whichever filling you decide to make, except that the tins required are different and so are the cooking times: bear this in mind before you start.

FOR THE PRUNES
- 500 g Agen prunes, organic if possible, stoned – if you like, but the stones help the prunes retain their flavour
- around 750 ml strong infusion Mahagastotte, Earl Grey or another aromatic tea
- peel of 1 lemon, shredded and blanched
- small stick cinnamon

Pour enough of the tea over the prunes to cover them and put in the lemon peel and the cinnamon. Simmer gently until the prunes are just tender, then remove the prunes from the liquid and put them into a bowl. Boil the liquid until it has caramelized and use it to coat the prunes.

Leave to cool.

For Filling 1, you will need a 23-cm loose-bottomed tart or sandwich tin, greased and floured.

For Filling 2, you will need a 20-cm non-stick spring-form cake tin, greased and floured.

- 200 g organic unbleached plain flour
- pinch of fine sea salt
- 1 rounded tablespoon vanilla caster sugar or plain caster sugar with ½ teaspoon vanilla extract
- ¼ teaspoon lemon zest
- 120 g unsalted butter, at room temperature
- 1 tablespoon (approximately) iced water

You can prepare the base by hand, but using a food-processor would be quicker.

Preheat the oven to 200°C/400°F/Gas Mark 6.

Combine the flour with the salt, sugar and lemon zest. Add the butter in small flakes and process intermittently until the mixture resembles coarse crumbs. Mix in the water and the vanilla extract, if using, with the machine running, but do not allow the mixture to get to ball stage – don't over-process. Drop the mixture on to a floured board and work it gently into a ball, then gently press it into a flattened round and wrap it in clingfilm. Refrigerate it for 30 minutes. Do not roll it out: instead work the dough evenly, with your hands lightly floured, into the sides of the tin and over the base, pressing out the bottom with your palm. Now either line the pastry with foil and freeze it for around 30 minutes before baking (which means you won't need to put any weight in the tin) or line it with greaseproof paper and pile in some baking beans. Put it into the oven and bake for 5–8 minutes, take it out and press down any air bubbles, then return it to the oven. For Filling 1, bake for another 15 minutes. For Filling 2, bake for another 12 minutes. Take it out and allow it to cool.

FOR FILLING I
- 400 g very fresh goat's cheese, e.g. Innes buttons, or Caprini Freschi, or French cheese from the Loire or Poitou, lightly drained or patted dry if it is rather moist, rind removed
- 2–3 tablespoons mascarpone
- 2–3 teaspoons vanilla sugar, or to taste as the cheese may be tart
- 2 teaspoons finely chopped thyme leaves
- ½ teaspoon lemon zest

Beat together all the ingredients until smooth, then spread the mixture in the cooked and cooled tart shell. Serve with the prunes on the side.

FOR FILLING 2
Goat's curd cheese is available from Highfields Farm Dairy in Staffordshire (Clifton Lane, Statford, Tamworth, Staffs B79 0AQ – tel: 01827 830197) or by ordering from specialist cheese shops.

- 2 large organic free-range eggs, separated
- 400 g fresh goat's curd cheese or soft goat's cheese, or a mixture of both, or Caprini Freschi, or soft cheeses from the Loire or Poitou, lightly drained or patted with paper towels if it is rather moist
- juice and zest of 1 lemon
- 2 level tablespoons ground almonds or cornflour
- 60 g unsalted light-tasting butter, melted
- 200 g mascarpone
- 100 g vanilla caster sugar

Preheat the oven to 180°C/350°F/Gas Mark 4.
   Put the egg yolks with all of the other ingredients, except the whites and the caster sugar, into a bowl and beat thoroughly into a thick cream. Whisk the egg whites until they are stiff, glossy peaks, then add the caster sugar a teaspoon at a time, whisking after each addition. Fold the meringue into the cream mixture, then pour it carefully into the pastry case in its tin. Put it into the oven for 45 minutes or until the top of the cake is evenly brown and feels firm to the touch. Turn off the oven and leave the

cake inside with the door closed for 10–15 minutes, then open the door a little way and leave it to cool completely. Take it out and release it from the tin. Serve it as it is with the prunes alongside, or top the cake with thick *crème fraîche*.

Tartine d'Amalfi

The lemons from Amalfi are exceptional. Just scratch the outside skin and sniff the heavenly scent. With the delicate buffalo ricotta from nearby Battipaglia – where water buffalo still roam the marshy plains – I have devised a version of lemon cheesecake with meringue topping that is the essence of tangy lightness.

FOR THE PASTRY CASE
- 250 g plain flour, sifted
- pinch of fine sea salt
- 165 g unsalted Charente butter in small pieces
- 1 heaped tablespoon vanilla-scented icing sugar
- 2 large organic egg yolks, mixed with 5 tablespoons iced spring water

FOR THE FILLING
- 8 eggs, separated
- 200 g caster sugar
- 100 g 40 per cent fat *fromage blanc* or mascarpone
- 150 g buffalo ricotta, or a very fresh cow's or sheep's milk ricotta, drained and sieved
- zest and juice of 2 large lemons, zest blanched, refreshed and dried
- 60 g icing sugar

Preheat the oven to 200°C/400°F/Gas Mark 6.

Put the flour and salt for the pastry into the food-processor bowl, drop in the butter and pulse until the mixture resembles breadcrumbs. Add the sugar, then pour in the egg mixture in a steady stream while the machine is running until the dough leaves the sides of the bowl. Or make the pastry by hand: rub the butter into the flour and salt, then make a well, pour in the egg mixture and mix to a dough. If made by hand, leave the pastry to rest for 30 minutes, use immediately if made in the food-processor.

Lightly butter and flour a 25-cm loose-bottomed deep tart tin and line it with the pastry. Prick the base, then line it with greaseproof paper weighted with baking beans. Bake for 12 minutes. Remove the paper and the beans, then bake for a further 5–6 minutes until a pale golden colour. Leave it to cool. Turn down the oven to 180°C/350°F/Gas Mark 4.

Now make the lemon filling. In a bowl whisk the egg yolks with the sugar until they are very creamy and smooth. This takes about 5 minutes with an electric whisk, or a little longer with a balloon whisk.

Fold in the *fromage blanc* or mascarpone and the ricotta, the lemon juice and zest. Whisk the egg whites, in a large clean mixing bowl that you have rubbed with a cut lemon, until they form stiff peaks, and carefully incorporate half into the egg and lemon mixture. Pour the lemon mixture into the pastry case and bake for around 20 minutes. Take it out and turn the oven to 220°C/450°F/Gas Mark 8.

To the reserved whisked egg whites add the icing sugar, teaspoon by teaspoon, beating to stiff peaks each time. Spoon over the cooked cake, making it look spiky, and return it to the oven on the middle shelf and bake until the meringue is pale gold. This should take just a few minutes so keep an eye on it. Allow the Tartine to cool before you take it out of the tin. Serve at room temperature, not chilled. For extra oomph pour Limoncello, lemon liqueur, into a ladle, heat it over a flame until it ignites, then pour it gently over the Tartine and serve.

Talmouses de Saint-Denis

I came across this recipe in an old cheese book, and although precise measures were not given, the gist was such that I could put it together. It's a sort of soufflé tart and the name derives from the ancient word *talmelier* meaning 'baker'. It became famous in the Saint-Denis area of Paris and the writer Balzac had a passion for it. It is rather rich, but my only concession to health would be to drink a glass of good red wine, such as a classic Bordeaux, with the tart. But that's my prescription for any rich-tasting savoury dish.

FOR THE FILLING

- 250 g fresh cream cheese
- 250 g Brie de Meaux or Camembert, rind removed
- a pinch of fine sea salt
- 10 g caster sugar
- 20 g plain flour, sieved
- 2 large organic free-range eggs, separated
- 2 large organic free-range egg yolks

FOR THE SEMI-SWEET SHORTCRUST PASTRY

- 250 g plain pastry flour
- a pinch of fine sea salt
- 175 g chilled Charente butter, in small pieces
- 1 level tablespoon icing sugar
- 2 medium organic free-range egg yolks, mixed with 5–6 tablespoons iced water

In a mixing bowl, or food-processor, beat together the cream cheese with the Brie de Meaux or Camembert until very fluffy and creamy white. Add the salt, the caster sugar and the flour and mix again, gently but thoroughly. In another bowl stir, but do not beat, all the egg yolks. Pour them into the cheese mixture, and blend with a spatula until smooth and velvety. Whisk the egg whites to frothy peaks and carefully incorporate them into the cheese mixture.

Preheat the oven to 180°C/350°F/Gas Mark 4.

Grease and flour 8 8-cm individual loose-bottomed tart tins.

Sift the flour and salt into the food-processor bowl and pulse with the butter until it resembles breadcrumbs. Add the icing sugar and pulse briefly. Then pour in the egg and water mixture slowly, with the motor running, being careful not to let the dough get too wet. Blend until it comes away from the sides of the bowl easily and is not sticky. Or make the pastry by hand: rub the butter and salt until it resembles breadcrumbs. Then make a well and stir in the egg and water mixture until the dough gathers into a ball and is not sticky. Rest the dough for 30 minutes if you make it by hand. Roll it out and use it to line the tartlet tins. Line the dough with greaseproof paper and weight it with baking beans, then bake blind for 8–10 minutes. Remove the paper and the beans and allow the tartlets to cool. Turn the oven up to 200°C/400°F/Gas Mark 6. Fill them with the cheese mixture, then return them to the oven and bake for 10–15 minutes or until the topping is golden and set.

Ricotta di Bufala al Caffè

Serves 4

This blend of creamy light buffalo milk ricotta with finely ground fresh coffee sounds rather bizarre but it is a real recipe from Campania. The coffee I prefer is from Florence and ground finely for the espresso machine from arabica coffees originating in Guatemala and Ethiopia. In fact, these wonderful coffee blends from Le Piantagioni del Caffè have helped keep my brain lively enough while I have been writing way into the depths of the night!

Whisk 250 g of very fresh sieved buffalo milk ricotta – if you can't get it try a very fresh cow's milk ricotta or a moist fresh cream cheese. In a separate bowl, mix 4 tablespoons of fresh finely ground coffee with 4 tablespoons of vanilla-scented icing sugar. Place the cheese in a nicely heaped mound and sprinkle over it the coffee-sugar mix, use a sieve or sugar shaker, then drizzle an Italian brandy, Strega or maybe even Amaretto around the edge. You could use Savoyarde sponge-finger biscuits to scoop up the cheese.

Caramels with Salted Butter

Not exactly a cheese recipe, but one that takes really good Charente butter – or an unpasteurized-milk farmhouse salted butter – and double *crème fraîche*. The caramels make melting velvety mouthfuls.

- 100 g icing sugar (sifted)
- 100 g pouring honey, such as acacia blossom, rhododendron or similar floral-scented honey
- 125 ml spring water

- 1 level tablespoon *crème fraîche*, thicker double style if possible
- 80 g salted butter, the best quality you can find

Put a heavy-bottomed saucepan on a heat-diffusing pad over a low heat and allow the icing sugar and honey to dissolve in 125 ml spring water. When the mixture is a lovely caramel colour take the saucepan off the heat. In another pan, bring the *crème fraîche* to just boiling point and stir it into the caramel. Put the pan back on a medium–low heat and cook until it reaches a thick coating consistency. Off the heat, beat in the butter. If you prefer firmer textured caramels heat the mixture for a little longer before you beat in the butter.

Butter a 15-cm sandwich cake tin and line it with waxed paper or baking parchment. Pour in the hot mixture and level it out with a spatula. When it is cool but still pliable, cut it with a sharp, clean knife into bite-sized cubes, then wrap them in waxed paper, or Cellophane, and store in an airtight tin.

Note: A tiny pinch of fine-grained salt in a vanilla custard sauce, such as Crème Anglaise, brings out the flavour of the vanilla beautifully.

A Travelling Tale

WALES

*M*any moons ago I used to drive to Wales to collect sheep's milk ice-cream. It was delicious, creamy, with the distinctive tang of sheep's milk and flavoured with fruits and essences, and was as fresh and vibrant as you can only achieve when using the best ingredients. The trick to keeping the ice-cream from melting was to wrap the packages in duvets, thereby insulating them for a few hours. I remember July and August 1991 as particularly hot, and my race against time as I hurtled down the M4 to get the bloomin' stuff back to base. The farm from which I bought the ice-cream was hidden away in a beautiful valley in mid-Wales where the sheep grazed on lush green undulating pastures and the lambs seemed to have springs on their hoofs as they bounced about in the sun.

The salty tang and a mineral impression is evident in cheeses like the Gorwydd, a traditional Caerphilly made by Todd Trethowan in Tregaron, Dyfed. It behaves well when it is ageing as it loves the attention of a cheese maturer, especially if the cellar has the cool dampness required to give its crust the velvety, downy mould, making it a very tactile cheese. It is delightful when eaten young and crumbly, with a fresh acidity to the taste. Maturity mellows the flavour, giving it a satisfying nuttiness. I have fond memories of a brief Welsh holiday when I spent days walking in fine drizzle beside rushing mountain streams, and picking wild salad leaves whose sharp bitterness was a perfect foil for Caerphilly cheese.

Sheep's Milk Ice-cream

- 200 g single cream
- 30 g lavender flowerheads
- 400 g sheep's milk yoghurt
- 80 g caster sugar

Warm the cream, put in the lavender flowers and leave them to infuse until you are satisfied that the taste is well defined. Strain the cream.

Blend all the ingredients in a sorbetière or ice-cream maker for 20 minutes. Alternatively, mix by hand, and put the bowl into the freezer. After 10 to 12 minutes stir the ice-cream to dissolve any ice crystals. The end result is a soft-scoop-style ice-cream.

As an alternative addition to lavender heads you could incorporate lightly toasted, skinned hazelnuts, crushed and combined with 2 table-spoons of Marsala.

Sheep's Milk Sorbet with Thyme

- 130 ml spring water
- 30 g liquid glucose – available from supermarkets
- 60 g caster sugar
- small bunch thyme sprigs, plus 1 tablespoon leaves
- 200 g sheep's milk *fromage frais*, or ricotta, sieved
- 200 g sheep's milk yoghurt

Heat together the first 3 ingredients until the sugar has dissolved, then put in the bunch of thyme, and leave it to infuse at a gentle simmer for 10 minutes. Strain it and let it cool completely. Stir the *fromage frais* and the yoghurt. Place in a sorbetière and churn for around 20 minutes. Alternatively put it into a plastic container and freeze. Stir the sorbet after about 10 minutes to disperse the ice crystals. When nearly set, stir in the fresh thyme leaves and return it to the freezer to set completely.

FRUIT AND CHEESE

Figs Wrapped in Fresh Vine Leaves Baked in a Fruit and Herb Syrup, Topped with Whipped Creamy Goat's and Sheep's Milk Cheeses and Mascarpone

Late August brings fat juicy figs and fresh vine leaves, which, when partnered with the rich-tasting fresh cheeses made with summer milk, produce flavours at their peak of perfection.

- 100 g caster sugar
- juice of 1 sweet orange, and rind, finely sliced, steeped in boiling water for 3 minutes, then drained and dried
- juice of ½ lemon
- 100 g unsalted butter, softened
- fresh bay leaf and fresh sage leaves
- 4 large purple-skinned figs, or 6 smaller ones – not too ripe
- 4–6 fresh vine leaves – they can be kept in the fridge or frozen
- fresh creamy cheeses of your choice – I would use a densely textured creamy Robiola di Langhe (3-milk variety), or Crescenza, or any earthy, rich, crumbly soft cheese with natural thin rippled rind; or Vignotte, or a young fresh goat's cheese, like Provençal Sariette de Banon, or fresh English or Irish goat's cheeses
- 2 tablespoons mascarpone
- 2–3 tablespoons almonds, lightly toasted, flaked

Bring the sugar, the orange and lemon juice to simmering point, stirring until the sugar has melted and the liquid has reduced slightly. Add the butter bit by bit, and whisk it as it melts into the syrup. Put in the bay leaf and sage leaves, then take the pan off the heat and leave it to infuse for an hour or two.

Preheat the oven to 180°C/350°F/Gas Mark 4.

Score the figs into 4 taking care not to cut all the way through. Spoon a small amount of the syrup into the middle of each, then wrap them carefully in the vine leaves and tie them with fine string. Place them side by side in a baking dish, and pour the rest of the syrup around them. Put the dish on the middle shelf of the oven, and bake for 15 minutes. The syrup should be bubbling gently. Take it out and leave it to cool to just warm. Open the vine leaves and spoon the syrup over the figs.

Whisk the fresh cheese(s) with the mascarpone to make a frothy topping and put a dollop on each fig. Scatter over some almonds. Flash under the grill for a few moments until the cheese starts to melt. Serve immediately.

Amare Saturn Peaches with Whipped Fromage Blanc and Mascarpone, and Crushed Amaretti Biscuits

Saturn peaches are small flattened peaches from Italy, which have a very short season from around the end of June to the end of July. Their taste is simple to describe: 'ambrosial nectar', and they are so sweet, so tender, that they barely need any adornment. For a quick dessert, skin them, by dipping them into boiling water for a minute or two, and sprinkle a squeeze of lemon juice over them to prevent the flesh going brown. Ease out the central stone, which is small and pliable. Sit the peaches on a plate. Whip up around 200 g of fresh *fromage blanc* and 200 g of mascarpone to a frothy mass, with a little vanilla-scented icing sugar if you feel it needs sweetening, and spoon a heaped mound into the centre of each peach. Scatter over some crushed Amaretti biscuits, and drizzle over a little Maraschino, or Strega, or Amaretti liqueur if you like. When the season for Saturn peaches ends you can always substitute them with the deeply sweet orange-fleshed Italian peaches, or the more elegant white-fleshed peaches. Essentially it is the overall taste of scented peaches with the delicate cream that etches the word summer into each mouthful.

Stuffed Dates

A very sixties retro mouthful, but delicious. It's most important to get the fattest, juiciest dates you can find rather than the puny-looking specimens in fancy boxes. Any good greengrocer or supermarket should have them, especially around Christmas when this recipe would come in handy for impromptu drinks or pigging out in front of the telly.

+ 80 g caster sugar
+ 2 tablespoons orange zest, blanched and then dried
+ 200 g very creamy cheese, such as Brillat Savarin, Explorateur, Finn, or a fresh creamy goat's or sheep's milk cheese
+ 80 g mascarpone
+ 150 g pistachio nuts, unsalted, and coarsely chopped

Put the sugar into a small saucepan with 2 tablespoons of water and heat until the sugar has dissolved. Add the orange zest and cook for a few minutes, then drain and let it cool. In a bowl mix the creamy cheese with the mascarpone, then fold in the candied orange peel and chopped pistachio nuts. Scoop a small amount of the cheese mixture into each date, and slightly close it. Eat as it is or, if you feel decadent and don't mind licking sticky fingers, drizzle a thin acacia honey over the top.

Very Fresh Tangy Goat's Cheese on Pain d'Épice with Rhubarb Compote or maybe a Smooth Mostarda d'Uva in the Style of Cogna

I prefer spring rhubarb to the forced January sticks, mainly because the flavour is softer and less acidic, and the colour is more vivid. And I can't think of a better Sunday lunch at this time of year than new season's milk-fed lamb roasted simply with rosemary and garlic (use the new plump, milky garlic cloves and don't peel them). For the last 10 minutes of the roasting time, turn the oven temperature very high and coat the meat with a dark runny Greek or chestnut honey to bubble and caramelize over the top. Follow that with rhubarb tart and *crème fraîche* – and my cheeks will be as pink as the 'barb and I'll be ready for a brisk walk over the Heath in Hampstead.

That is the more traditional route. However, fresh spring goat's milk cheeses teamed with rhubarb are also a delight, after all the tough winter weather. Fuel food makes way for fresher tastes, when new grass imparts an astringency to milk and cheeses have a cleansing sharpness on the palate. That's one of the joys of cheese – you can taste the seasons in them.

Thinly slice some *pain d'épice* or a simple spice or ginger cake that's gone a bit stale. Fry it in unsalted butter until crisp, then pat dry on paper towels. Slice a very fresh button goat's cheese – try Innes buttons from Staffordshire – or a very fresh French, Italian or Spanish goat's cheese. Make 3 thin rounds and lay them on top of the fried cake.

For the *compote*, chop 300 g rhubarb into 2-cm chunks, and poach it in 125 g unsalted butter with malty Muscovado sugar to taste and a split vanilla pod for 10–15 minutes. Turn off the heat and leave it to cool. Remove the vanilla pod. Serve the rhubarb lukewarm with the cheese-topped cake. If you don't have anything like the cakes mentioned above, you could crush some biscuits – choose semi-sweet oat ones like Hobnobs – and mix them with melted butter. Remould them into rounds and dry out in the oven at 200°C/400°F/Gas Mark 6 for 5 minutes. Let them cool before topping them with the cheese.

If you come across *mostarda* in Italy, or at your delicatessen, look for the variety not made with mustard oil, from Cremona, but the dark jam-like one in the old-style Cogna way with grape must, or *vinaccia*, which is the residue left after the grapes have been pressed for winemaking. A wine-producer acquaintance in Monforte d'Alba in the heart of the Piedmont once, very graciously, let me scoop some grape must into a container to take home with me, as I love coating very fresh creamy cheeses with this crunchy, fruity, winy substance.

If you can't find this *mostarda* in your local deli, look for a hand-made chutney – there are numerous small producers who use really good ingredients. If you can find one consisting of apples, pears, walnuts and spices, add a little port or red wine to give it added finesse. A spoonful served with fresh cheeses, or a tangy crumbly Wensleydale, Lancashire or

Cheshire, or a rich textural sheep's cheese such as Ossau from the Pyrenees or Pecorino from Tuscany or Sardinia, or even a medium-matured Berks-well from the West Midlands, turns the cheese course into the dessert too. Even a velvety creamy blue like Gorgonzola would harmonize beautifully.

A Travelling Tale

IRELAND

When I was in Ireland I noticed how close the clouds were to the land. I felt as though I could almost touch them, which made me think that Ireland must be closer to heaven than anywhere else.

If the drizzling rain in Wales has a sharp sting as it lashes against your face then Ireland's is soft and gentle as its fine mist of spray caresses your skin. The water from mountain streams babbles rather than chatters, and the ground underfoot is mossy and padded like a goosedown jacket. I've been to Dingle Bay and walked along the beach in the footsteps of Ryan's daughter and downed a pint of Guinness at the local – it was pure nectar, nothing like the stuff you get in British bars. Some of the best meals I've ever had were at a small restaurant-cum-gallery on the Isle of Valentia not far from Dingle, where the seafood chowder and poached salmon were sublime, as was the porter fruit cake I enjoyed, with a strong crumbly Irish Cheddar. I eat it now with Bill Hogan's masterpieces: Gabriel and Desmond cheeses. If you're ever anywhere near Schull in Co. Cork look him up – you can get directions from the post office. He's a bit of a charmer and really enjoys introducing customers to his cheeses, which are made in the Swiss Gruyère style, and he makes a superb fondue.

The cheeses from Ireland are some of the most interesting I've seen or tasted. They have a richness and quality like French cheeses but there are also many that resemble Dutch or Italian styles. Look out for Durrus, Ardrahan, Gubbeen, Coolea, Cashel Blue, Mine Gabhar and Cooleeney.

Porter Cake with Sour Cherries

- 250 g unsalted Échire butter, or similar, at room temperature
- 440 g self-raising flour, sifted
- 440 g fine brown sugar (light muscavado)
- 440 g seedless raisins – Lexia, if possible
- 250 g sultanas
- 125 g dried sour cherries – soak them in a little warm water to reconstitute them
- 125 g almonds, blanched and roughly chopped
- 125 g chopped mixed peel
- zest of 1 lemon, blanched then dried
- pinch of mixed spice
- 250 ml Guinness
- 4 free-range organic eggs
- 1 level teaspoon bicarbonate of soda

Preheat the oven to 140°C/275°F/Gas Mark 1.

Either by hand or in a food-processor, cut the butter into small nuggets and rub it into the sieved flour. Then add the rest of the dry ingredients. Blend thoroughly together – but do not use the sharp blade of the food-processor. Warm the Guinness and pour it into a bowl. Dissolve the bicarbonate of soda in a little of it. Beat the eggs into the Guinness, then add the bicarbonate of soda. Then stir the Guinness mixture into the dry ingredients. Grease and line a 22.5-cm loose-bottomed cake tin with baking parchment and turn the mixture into it. Cover the top with a circle of greaseproof paper, and bake for 3–3½ hours. Remove the paper from the top for the last 30 minutes. Test the cake with a skewer to make sure it's cooked: if the skewer comes out clean it's done. If not leave the cake for a little longer and try again. Serve with a strong, crumbly farmhouse Cheddar, or Lancashire or hard crumbly Irish cheese like the Gabriel or Desmond.

SPECIAL OCCASIONS AND CHEESE FANTASIES

Terrine of Beaufort

Beaufort cheese is the Prince of French Gruyères, and one of my favourite cheeses. Normally I wouldn't want to cook with it, since its floral, fruity flavours make it perfect at the end of a meal with a glass of fruity white wine. However, here is a rather swanky recipe; it requires a little extra effort, but the result is worth it. It is also useful to note that the addition of Beaufort to a fondue will give it extra depth and richness.

Serves 6
- 300 g Beaufort (the winter cheese will be less sweet and nutty than the *alpage* summer cheese)
- 1 tablespoon Vin de Savoie, or other light, fruity white wine
- 6 small artichokes, with purple tips to the leaves, if possible, or 3 medium sweet potatoes, white-fleshed rather than orange
- 1 tablespoon lemon juice
- 1 tablespoon plain flour
- 25 g unsalted butter, for cooking with the artichokes, or 25 g butter and a pinch of nutmeg, if using sweet potatoes
- 24 thin slices *pancetta*, without rind, or 6 thin slices *prosciutto*
- 3 medium egg yolks
- 1½ tablespoons milk
- 125 g *crème fraîche*
- sea salt and black pepper

- fresh organic free-range eggs, soft-poached
- soft salad leaves, such as watercress, lamb's lettuce

Cut the cheese into small dice and place in a bowl with the wine to marinate. Next remove the leaves of the artichokes to reveal the hearts. Place the hearts in 1 litre of simmering water with the lemon juice, flour and butter, and cook until tender – but don't overboil them or they will blacken. If using the sweet potatoes, steam them with their skins on until they are tender. Remove the skins, slice and toss them carefully in butter and nutmeg.

Preheat the oven to 180°C/350°F/Gas Mark 4. Take a non-stick 26-cm terrine (if you haven't a non-stick one, butter whatever you do have) and line it with the *pancetta* and *prosciutto*, making sure the ham overlaps the sides.

Put the egg yolks into a bowl and mix well, adding the milk and *crème fraîche* with a little salt and pepper. Add the Beaufort to the egg mixture. Place a thin layer of Beaufort mixture, then a layer of artichoke or sweet potato, cover with a layer of Beaufort, then a second layer of artichoke or sweet potato, then another layer of Beaufort before bringing the ends of the ham over the terrine to cover. Cover with foil and cook for 1 hour. Remove from the oven and allow the terrine to cool before placing it in the fridge overnight or for at least 12 hours. You may want to strain off any excess fat.

About 10 minutes before you wish to serve, poach 1 small egg per person in simmering water for 2 minutes. Drain on paper towel and reserve. Unmould the terrine, slice it into 6 serving portions and place on individual serving plates. Flash them under the grill to toast the cheese slightly. Serve the watercress and soft leaf salad alongside with the poached egg on top, lightly sprinkled with a little coarse sea salt. Dress the salad, if you wish, with a small amount of Dijon mustard mixed with some chicken stock.

Fourme au Sauterne

Fourme d'Ambert macerated with Sauterne wine. Mash, not too smoothly, 200 g Fourme d'Ambert blue cheese from the Auvergne – although you could use a young, creamier-style Stilton – and mix with enough Sauterne to make a thick dropping paste. Cover the bowl tightly with clingfilm and refrigerate for 2 days. Mix thoroughly and serve with thin wafer cheese biscuits or sticks of celery and cucumber as a dip with aperitifs. If you wish, add a tablespoon of *crème fraîche* for a creamier taste.

Brie aux Noix

Take a wedge of Brie de Meaux and carefully slice through it horizontally so you have two identical triangles – a cheese wire or a knife with a long thin blade, such as a fish-filleting knife, makes this job easier. With the soft pâte uppermost spread over one triangle a mixture of *crème fraîche*, *mascarpone* and toasted, roughly chopped walnuts. Sandwich the cheese together and press down gently. If possible, use fresh walnuts: crack them open, then roughly break them up and toast them in the oven. Serve on its own at the end of a meal or as part of a larger cheese selection.

Brie aux Truffes

As for Brie aux Noix, but this time a thin layer of *crème fraîche* and shavings of black truffles – fresh, if possible, or use the ones in jars – then, very judiciously, sprinkle over truffle oil. Sandwich the cheese together and press down gently. Serve as for Brie aux Noix.

Camembert au Roquefort et aux Noix

Split a ripe but not too ripe farmhouse Camembert horizontally into 2 discs. In a bowl, mash 80–100 g Roquefort with a splash of Cognac or Armagnac, then fold in a little *crème fraîche* and roughly chopped walnuts. Spread it over one of the Camembert discs and carefully sandwich with the other on top. Press down gently. Prepare this at least 2 hours before serving.

Coeur de Camembert au Calvados

Choose a milder-style Camembert, ripe but not with an overpowering aroma. Scrape off and cut away the white bloomy crust as best you can to reveal the cheese. Dip the cheese in Pommeau – an aperitif with Calvados added – or Calvados mixed with a little sweet apple juice or cider until it is well soaked, then transfer it to a plate of fine dry biscuit crumbs, in the style of Petit Beurre or Rich Tea, to coat it. Place a half walnut on top of the cheese or a slice of poached sweet apple and leave for a couple of hours for the flavours to mingle.

Richesse de Fromage

Triple cream cheese topped with Lexia raisins soaked in dessert wine. Choose a cheese like Explorateur, or Elmhirst from Sussex, weighing around 200 g. It must be very fresh, without a bloomy rind. In a bowl, marinate Lexia or other plump, juicy raisins in a dessert wine for at least 2 hours or overnight. (I have also used dried sour cherries soaked in cherry brandy.) Place a layer of drained marinated fruit on top of the cheese, and artistically drizzle over some of the marinade. This turns the cheese course into the dessert too.

Gorgonzola Torte

Rich Gorgonzola cremificato layered with mascarpone and fresh basil leaves. Line a sieve (not the conical type), that has a medium-sized mesh, with sterilized muslin overlapping the container. Layer slices of Gorgonzola *dolce cremificato*, then mascarpone, then a scattering of roughly torn basil leaves until you come to the top of the sieve. You should finish with a layer of mascarpone. You should have 3 layers of Gorgonzola and 3 of mascarpone. Put the muslin over the cheese. Place a lid or saucer on top and weight it to compress the layers. The sieve should be over a bowl as the excess liquid from the cheese and mascarpone will squeeze through the muslin. Refrigerate for at least 2 hours. Gently release the Torte from the container on to a plate. Cover the cheese with more mascarpone and place fresh basil leaves to decorate the mound. Cut it into wedges. Serve with thin slices of walnut bread.

Camembert Toasts

Roast some walnuts and grate them finely. Cut white bread into medium-thick slices and toast on one side. Top the untoasted side with Camembert, no crust, creamed with a little *fromage blanc*. Cover it with the finely grated walnuts and cut the slices into triangles. Place them on a non-stick baking sheet and bake at 200°C/400°F/Gas Mark 6 for 5 minutes or until the walnut topping is toasted. Serve as an aperitif or as a simple starter.

GREAT BRITISH CHEESES

There have always been good British cheeses, and in the ten years since I started my business I have seen a resurgence of farmhouse-made cheeses that has put Britain back on track as a force to be reckoned with. The British climate cannot compete with Provence or Tuscany in the summer, and the countryside lacks high-altitude mountain pastures for cattle to graze. But we do have lush, undulating meadows in Somerset, Wales and Scotland where cattle produce rich, buttery milk for hard, sharp-tasting cheeses.

There is nothing to beat a farmhouse Cheddar from Somerset, whether it is from George Keen in Wincanton, whose cheeses have a slightly pitted crumbly texture and distinctive taste with a sharp sting as it warms in the mouth, or from Jamie Montgomery in North Cadbury, a closer-textured, more mellow, nutty-tasting cheese, sophisticated on the palate. These are cheeses of such high quality and superb craftsmanship that they can be served on their own at the end of the meal with a crisp dessert apple and a glass of fine Bordeaux without any other adornment. If cheese is royal then Cheddar of this quality is king.

Out of all the blue cheeses, Stilton is in favour throughout the year. Our preferred one is made in Colston Bassett near Nottingham at a small independent dairy. It responds happily to our maturing methods. I want Stilton to have that lovely biscuit roughness to the outside crust while inside the blue should be well dispersed and the cheese should crumble but still have a moist creaminess. The taste should not be too bitter but should have strength and guts. After a few weeks in our cheese room, which is cool but with good humidity, the flavours of the cheeses round out. They are quite different from pre-packed supermarket specimens.

Whenever we leave out Stilton tasters on the counter, customers are surprised when I tell them what they're eating: they always say they thought it was a continental cheese.

It is all too easy to take our cheeses for granted, to pop a block of Cheddar into your shopping trolley at the supermarket and grate it over everything. But there are real discoveries to be made, not only with traditional cheeses but also with the newer ones like Waterloo, Wigmore, Celtic Promise, Stinking Bishop, Innes buttons, Woolsery, Tymsboro, Ticklemore, Flower Marie, Golden Cross and Harbourne Blue or the hand-made farmhouse cheeses of Sue Proudfoot at Whalesborough Farm near Bude in North Cornwall and Pam Rodway's excellent sweet milk and Califer cheeses from Wester Laurenceton Farm in Morayshire. These are all stars in their own right, and there are many others for you to discover. However, you will have to search out real cheese shops and I have listed those that I think are worth a visit on page 197.

Although I keep many continental cheeses, I apply the same methods to maturing British cheeses, albeit with a few modifications to take into account the style and fabrication of the product. The artisan-made cheeses respond to our maturing methods sometimes almost instantly, at other times with a little coaxing. What always transpires is a wakening of potential for improvement and a development of structure and taste that not only delights me but surprises our customers.

British cheese has become sophisticated and stylish, able to stand shoulder to shoulder with its continental counterparts. Long may it continue and strive for greatness.

PLANNING YOUR OWN CHEESE AND WINE TASTING

Have a list of the wines and cheeses you are offering, with tasting notes, which you can ask your friendly cheesemonger and wine merchant to help you with. If this is not possible, use the tasting notes I have made throughout the book to work out what cheeses you would like to offer and the types of wine to go with them. It is useful to remember that you want the tastes to evolve from mild to stronger, and most strident at the end. Take into account the seasonal varieties available, and whether any guests have special dietary requirements (for example, a pregnant woman may prefer to eat only pasteurized cheese). I once gave a tasting with Anthony Hanson, a distinguished, respected wine buyer and Master of Wine, for a group of enthusiastic imbibers eager to learn more about matching wine and cheese.

To get them started we served a sparkling wine, Crémant de Bourgogne Brut Cave de Lugny – or you could choose a *prosecco* or *blanc de blanc*, with a three-year-aged Parmigiano Reggiano. This was a bold start, as champagne-style wines are notoriously difficult to match with food. Parmigiano is sharp, gritty, but also melting and mellow as it breaks down, and partners a dry fizzy wine perfectly. Or try a Comté from the Jura, or a Tomme d'Abondance from Savoie, or maybe a tangy farmhouse Cheshire, which has been clothbound and matured for at least 5–6 months. A young Camembert or Brillat Savarin may also be considered.

We chose four wines, two reds and two whites, matched to the following cheeses.

For the hard cheese, there was a classic red Bordeaux, Château Ballat-Berguin Bordeaux Supérieur CB 1997, with a farmhouse unpasteurized fifteen-month-matured Cheddar. The nutty taste becomes full and fruity as it warms in the mouth and a dry classic wine like this livens up the flavours.

We served a Sauvignon *blanc*, Touraine Sauvignon, Château de la Presle 1999, with goat's cheese, Sainte Maure de Touraine, from the Loire. The fruity mineral flavours of the wine perfectly accented this cheese. Or try it with Sancerre.

Then came Fougeru, a small-sized Brie with a rich, creamy texture; its thick depth prevents the heart of the cheese becoming totally ripened, which enhances the flavour. The soft outer edges and slightly crumbly centre have an earthy but rather mossy taste, with a delightful mushroom aroma. Fruity red wines from the Gamay grape go well with it, such as Beaujolais, or maybe a warmer spiced Côtes du Rhône. We chose Domaine Ste-Anne Côtes du Rhône Villages 1998.

Matching a blue cheese can be a problem, as the aggressive flavours sometimes overpower wine. However, a wine such as St Émilion or Montus Madiran with a rich, powerful, tannin flavour will stand up to it, or you could try a dessert wine, such as Sauterne or Muscat, especially with Roquefort. At the cheese tasting I served a Fourme d'Ambert, because its broad-textured 'fatty' paste had a nuttiness to its blue veining, making it suitable for tasting with different cheeses, and with a southern Rhône wine like Vacqueyras or Côtes du Rhône Villages. However, we drank with it a not too sweet Loire wine, Le Domaine Richou 1997 Coteaux de L'Aubance Sélection, with just enough spice and tropical fruits to mellow the blue tang. It was a revelation, the star of the event.

For the washed-rind cheese I chose Époisses, because the time of year – mid-June and not too hot – meant that the cheese was stunning: moist, aromatic, rich and mellow. The flavours mingled perfectly and aligned exactly with Côtes du Rhône Villages. However, you could always go for the wild option of a robust Marc de Bourgogne if you wanted to turn up the volume of your tastebuds (not for the fainthearted!).

My last cheese was what I call the Oddity, mainly because its coating with herbs, spices or even truffles is difficult to match with wine. It was a firm-textured goat's cheese, covered in herbs, peppercorns and dried chillies (rather like the coating of the Corsican cheese Brin d'Amour), called Préfailles, from the Pays Nantais in France. The taste was quite light for a hard goat's cheese but sufficiently fruity for both white and red wines, not too dry or sharp. We chose a white Mâcon Uchizy 1999 from Raphaël and Gérard Sallet: with its dry, fresh-tasting citrus tang and earthy bite, it aligned well with the herbs and spices surrounding the cheese.

Serve dry water biscuits, too, unless you want to make your tasting more substantial, when you could offer assorted breads, thinly sliced, with an unsalted butter, for those who must have it, and various types of savoury biscuits, from oatcakes to wafers and crackers. If you want a fresh crunchy taste, such as celery, apples or grapes, go ahead, but I feel they detract from the seriousness of the tasting. Perhaps there should be some chilled natural spring water to sip between wines, but don't let your guests gulp down huge amounts of water with cheeses: they aren't the best of friends in the digestion department.

You could also explore the vast array of Italian or Spanish cheeses and wines. I find Australian wines too aromatic to partner cheeses – except, of course, the more expensive ones with depth and character. English and Irish cheeses are perfect with French wines, but vary the selection of British cheeses so that there aren't too many of the same texture. Search out the softer cheeses, such as Wigmore and Waterloo from Berkshire, or Bath Soft, or a well-cared-for Cornish Yarg with soft, buttery edges. There is also a Gloucestershire cheese called Stinking Bishop, named after the type of pear used in the *eau de vie* Poire William in which the cheese is washed. If it has been carefully matured the flavour will be rich and melting, perfect for fruity ripe wines or a dry Jurançon. There are some lovely Scottish cheeses too, especially a goat's cheese called Califer from Morayshire, with a dry, nutty, crumbly texture often found in Loire cheeses. I would steer clear of trying to match wines with smoked cheeses because the flavour of both wine and cheese are killed stone dead.

For interesting wine lists see wine magazines such as *Decanter*, or ask at your local wine warehouse, or even your supermarket, if they have a resident wine manager.

WHITE WINE WITH CHEESE? WHY NOT?

For many, the only cheese to serve with white wine is a mild goat's cheese. However, as soon as you taste cheeses such as Maroilles and Munster, or even the Irish Durrus and Gubbeen, or a washed-rind British cheese, such as Stinking Bishop, the picture becomes clearer. The spicy aromatic Gewürztraminer partners Munster to a T. Riesling, with its slightly sweet yet earthy taste, can pose an interesting foil for Maroilles, whose strength and bite would destroy other wines. Somehow the soft fruit and mellow citrus tang balance the richer flavours and pungent aromas of cheeses from Alsace and other areas of north-east France.

Riesling is not a fashionable wine although it is much loved by wine connoisseurs and writers, and I expect it's because the 'nose' on the first impact imparts a rather earthy citric farmyard aroma. Yet its flavours are fresh and zingy. But I love Gewürztraminer, with its aroma of old roses and musky honey taste. It's my favourite wine at the start of a meal, or when I'm serving only Alsace cheeses. Look out for the Rolly Gassman labelled wines as they have a particularly high concentration of fruit.

Alsace wines have never had the same impact on the wine-buying public as, say, Bordeaux, Loire or Burgundy. I suppose it's because the bottle and the design of the labels have a rather old-fashioned, stolid appearance, and look more German than French. I once had a long involved discussion with fellow pupils and tutor at a wine class I attended as to whether Alsace winemakers should redesign their bottles and labelling to make them more appealing to the younger market. After all, we are living in an age where marketing and design can be a make or break for many businesses and products. Similarly, the Swiss Dairy Corporation is just as concerned about the way their cheeses are viewed – rather on the old-fashioned, solid and dependable side instead of being upbeat and partnered with modern ingredients. They are subtly bringing their logo up to date, to make it more appealing to the younger market eager for new tastes and recipes that are easy to prepare. Should Alsace winemakers think along the same lines?

I hate to bring up the question of price, as there are so many so-called 'bargains' to be had – or have you been 'had' in the process? Please take into account that before a wine reaches Britain there are the costs of making and bottling the wine, transporting it from the winemaker to its place of destination; then there are the import duty and shipper's expenses, the VAT, and that's before the shop has added their margin. A wine retailing at £2.99 has therefore probably cost barely 30p to make. Taking this into account, you have to expect flavours that have had a little help from chemical rather than natural ingredients. If you pay a little more – say around £6 – you will get more for your money and a better introduction to the fascinating world of wine.

Here are some more favourite wines – sourced for the shop to partner cheese:

◆ White
Lugana, Lake Garda, northern Italy: crisp, fresh and tangy – perfect with seafood, and with monastery-made cheese, such as Mont des Cats, or Bel Paese-style cheeses, and smooth-textured semi-hard cheeses with a not-too-rich or complex flavour.

Arneis, Piedmont, northern Italy: Roberto Sarotto's delicious earthy, light-textured classic wine with a gentle fizz on the nose. Lovely as an aperitif with cubes of young Montasio or Asiago cheese, or perhaps a young Caerphilly, or crumbly nutty goat's cheeses such as Sainte-Maure or Crottin de Chavignol. Cheeses made with a mixture of milks like the Piedmontese Robiola di Langhe will also be well matched, as the texture of the three-milk cheese is rich and fudgy while the sheep and cow's milk version has a thin bloomy rind and inside a smooth fluid texture, not unlike Brie. It tastes nutty but not too strong.

Chignin, Savoie, eastern France: René Quenard's La Maréchale wine is perfect for Fondue and Raclette, as well as young fruity cheeses such as Beaufort and Reblochon. A clean, refreshing herbal taste. The *Chignin Bergeron* wine is from the lower slopes where the vines ripen in more sheltered warmth. This is the perfect wine for Vacherin Mont d'Or, with its delicate perfume masking a full-bodied fruity wine of juicy intensity.

Savoie wines are rarely seen outside their region, which is a shame since they are real discoveries when partnered with cheeses of the region too, such as Comté, Morbier, and all the different goat's and sheep's milk cheeses.

Château Bouscassé, Gascony, south-west France: Alain Brumont's wines are always well structured and full of interesting flavours. This has a fresh citrus zesty taste, perfect for fish and seafood, and the fresh lemon tang of young goat's cheese.

Château Montus, Pacherenc du Vic Bihl Sec, Gascony, south-west France: a deliciously aromatic dry wine with a citrus zest and grassy aromas. Try it with oysters and a fresh cream cheese dip made with finely chopped herbs and a little minced garlic.

Sancerre, Chavignol, Loire: Pascal Thomas's flinty earthy classic wine is the desired accompaniment for the local goat's cheese, Crottin de Chavignol. English goat's cheeses, such as Mary Holbrook's truncated pyramid, or a semi-mature log with a crumbly fresh tang, will also match.

Vermentino Bianco, from the hillside vineyards Lorieri. Made with the single grape variety from old vines in Apuana, Tuscany. The taste is deep and rich like an aged Burgundy.

◆ Rosé
Rosé de Béarn, Château de la Motte, south-west France: Michel Arrat's stunning smoky, warm and floral-scented wine. A surprising reawakening of the joy of rosé. A summer stunner to partner a mozzarella, tomato and basil salad. Or tear open the leaf wrapping of a Banon from Provence and scoop out the spicy soft cheese for a real taste of heat and strength. A gentler taste will be the slim log Sariette de Banon with the traditional sprig of summer savory (*sariette*) on top.

◆ Red
Gamay, Savoie, eastern France: René Quenard's fruity light-textured wine in the classic Beaujolais style, and perfect for all Savoie cheeses and cooked

cheese recipes, as well as Brie de Meaux, Camembert and soft cheeses with white bloomy rinds such as Olivet Cendrée from Orléannais, triple-cream Brillat Savarin, which has been allowed to ripen for a week or two, or a semi-matured Chaource from the Champagne region.

Vermentino Rosso: from the rare old vines situated high on the hills overlooking Massa in Apuana, Tuscany. Bold, full-bodied, robust and spicy. Serve alongside Pecorino.

Merlot, Vin de Pays des Côtes de Gascogne: Alain Brumont celebrated the millennium with a special *cépage*. One of the most drinkable wines with all foods, this one is rich, chewy and robust. Partner with a young semi-hard sheep's cheese from the Pyrenees, a British cheese made with sheep's milk, Spenwood from Berkshire, or a young Berkswell from the west Midlands – or, indeed, a new season's Pecorino from Tuscany.

Château Montus Madiran, Gascony, south-west France: a stunning full-bodied rich-flavoured wine for partnering robust meat dishes such as beef, game and especially *cassoulet* and *confit de canard*. The cheese to partner it would be Époisses, Ami Chambertin or a fully matured Comté d'Estive or other Gruyère-style cheeses, Cantal Mont-Grêle, the Auvergne Cheddar-style cheese but with a more spicy bite, and blue cheeses, such as Cashel Blue with its rich, buttery, fatty texture and nutty blue veins, as well as not-too-mature Picos de Europa from León in Spain, which will taste strong and have a creamy richness enhanced by the vine leaves wrapped around the cheese.

Coteaux du Tricastin, southern Rhône: Delas Frères' deliciously spicy dark blackcurrant wine from the Grenache grape, appealing to all food styles, and mountain cheeses including St Marcellin, a small disc of rich-tasting cow's milk with a thin rind and natural bloomy moulds of white and blue.

Château de Beaulieu, Marmande, Agen: Robert Schulte's dry, classy wine, perfect with Cheddar-style cheeses, Stilton and, of course, rare roast beef, or festive stuffed turkey.

Sangiovese della Daunia, Puglia, Italy: organic wine with a dry, soft, fruity taste and easy-drinking appeal. Light crumbly cheeses would be an interesting foil.

Côte de Beaune, *Nuits St Georges* or *Pommard* are recommended wines from a sommelier friend of mine, as they partner washed-rind cheeses such as Époisses, Ami Chambertin, Maroilles, and other cheeses that have a pungent aroma, but a deceptively mellow taste.

Côte Rôtie, *Bordeaux* or *Pauillac*: are favoured with a ripe Camembert, and other cheeses with smooth textures and earthy flavours.

Chianti Colli Fiorentini, Tuscany, Italy: typical classic simple-style Chianti to partner a plate of spaghetti topped with shavings of Pecorino.

Santenay, Closé de la Confrérie, Domaine Vincent Girardin: I have been a long-time admirer of this young winemaker, whose enthusiasm, energy and total commitment produce distinctive wines to drink young or lay down for a year or two (if you can restrain yourself). Burgundy of this class – rich, classic and superbly well constructed – encapsulates what wine-drinking is all about. Enjoy with fine cheeses, especially the local Époisses. Expensive but worth it.

Côtes du Vivarais, Ardèche: the region is a well-known holiday destination, and the creamy goat's and cow's milk cheeses are renowned in France. This is a delicious wine which has received many awards, and the taste will not only bring back happy holiday memories but will partner well-flavoured fish and meat dishes as well as the more pungent goat's cheeses.

Valpolicella, Veneto, Italy: no visit to Lake Garda would be complete without tasting the wonderful local wine. Its dry, fruity tang from the local grapes, Corvina, Rondinella and Molinara, makes this a match for Montasio, Asiago and Vezzena as well as aged Pecorino.

Magliano, Tuscany, Italy: a 'super' Tuscan with enough age in the bottle to give it a real, classy taste. Rather voluptuous with a heady intensity. Partner it with sheep's cheese, aged or rich and soft.

Enrico I, Piedmont, Italy: a stylish wine with classic traditional rich Barolo taste. This estate is run on traditional lines and a full-bodied wine like this would partner robust-flavoured cheeses.

Barbera d'Asti, Piedmont, Italy: luscious darkly fruity wine with violet and berry flavours, and warm generous tones. Sautéed wild mushrooms, like porcini, or meat dishes with rich wine sauces partner wines like this, as well as strong full-flavoured cheeses such as farmhouse-matured Fontina, Taleggio and Gorgonzola.

♦ Dessert, Semi-Sweet Wines, Champagne and New World Wines

Pacherenc de Vendemiaire, south-west France: dessert wine with a sweet spicy taste. Look out for the one dated December or January on the label, and partner it with Pyrenees sheep's cheeses, or blue cheeses such as Roquefort (look for the Carles label), Fourme d'Ambert or Beenleigh Blue (sheep's milk), from Totnes in Devon, Harbourne Blue (goat's milk) and Devon Blue (cow's milk).

Château de Cerons: a classic Sauterne and perfect for strong-flavoured blue cheeses, such as Roquefort or a Stilton that has had careful handling in the maturing room. The texture should be buttery and rich, and the blue strident but not aggressive.

Champagne Vilmart from Rilly: a classic well-structured champagne with a dry but foamy vanilla essence to the taste is delightful with Chaource from the same region; Langres, a washed orange sticky rind with a smoky mellow taste and creamy texture; Elmhirst, a double-cream cheese from Somerset with an earthy mushroom taste; Comté d'Estive, with its characteristic nutty Gruyère style, a soft young triple-cream Brillat Savarin, or a young Camembert.

The sharper, crumbly English cheeses match a stylish beer – made by one of the new style micro-breweries – as do the incredibly spicy cheeses of northern France, such as Boulette d'Avesnes or Maroilles. Or try them with Kirsch or schnapps. A glass of good whisky with Cheshire is appetizing.

The Normandy cheeses such as Pont l'Évêque, Livarot, and Trappist monastery cheeses such as Mont des Cats, are delicious with farmhouse-style ciders in summer, as are British cheeses Celtic Promise, Double Gloucester, Cheddar or a semi-matured Bath Soft.

Australian and New Zealand wines can have rather too much scented oak to partner cheese successfully. However, I am finding more wines that provide the necessary depth of flavour to flatter and complement cheese, perhaps because cheesemaking is becoming increasingly important in Australia and New Zealand. I have tasted delicious blue cheeses, such as Gippsland from Victoria, as well as their very creamy rich Brie, a lovely sheep's cheese called Meredith from the Western District of Victoria, and Milawa washed-rind cheese from Australia's old wine region Hunter Valley.

Look for white wines with a refreshing acidity to partner goat's cheeses and other fresh cheese. For the Camembert-style cheese or others with a bloomy white rind, think of the more matured Chardonnay for a white wine, and light Pinot Noir or Semillon as the red option. For washed-rind cheeses, vintage champagne is lovely with a young cheese, but for the more matured varieties look for full-bodied Pinot or Grenache. Blue cheeses would match the sweet Muscat wines as well as red wines from Barossa, which are matured in small barrels with a high alcohol level and therefore a natural sweetness coming through. For semi-hard cheeses look for full-bodied red wines with that familiar tart tannin finish such as Cabernet Sauvignon or Shiraz, and for hard cheeses search out the fortified sweet wines, even a sweet sherry, and, of course, a well-knit matured red wine, with a full rounded balanced taste.

CHEESE WITH . . .

Fresh Fruit

Brian Haw of Academy Fruits always selects varieties of apple or pear from Brogdale Horticultural Trust that perfectly accompany cheese. In season the plums are equally delicious and we can't wait to slice a piece of Gruyère, Brie or Cheshire to compare notes. Eating apples such as Kent, Egremont, Cox, and honey-tasting old-fashioned pears with exotic French names alongside English, French, Italian, and Irish cheeses turn a dessert into a meal. Brian's fruit 'cheeses' or pastes, made with quince, plum, blackcurrant or a mixture, are not overly sweet but have the intense fruitiness with the scent of the fruit alive and active on the palate. A fruit cheese with a strong hard cheese or very fresh cream cheese is a lovely way to end a meal.

Vegetables, Olives, Nuts

With a little culinary imagination we can enhance their natural affinity to cheese.

Olives

Stuff large queen-size green Cerignola olives either with roughly chopped sheep's milk feta tossed in finely chopped mint and olive oil, or with creamy sheep's or goat's milk cheese mashed with fresh herbs such as oregano, thyme and fennel fronds.

Nuts

Nuts, whether fresh new season varieties, or roasted, fried and aromatized with spices such as paprika, can be tossed with cheese for a salad, sandwiched into a Brie or Camembert or served as an appetizer with cubes of salty feta. Wet walnuts enhance strong-flavoured cheeses like Parmesan and Pecorino.

Pickled Cucumbers

A traditional Eastern European crunchy vegetable condiment that works well with hard and soft cheeses. Whether visiting the weekend farmers' market in Belgrade or the pickle man on Delancey Street in downtown Manhattan, the sight of large wooden barrels filled to the brim with knobbly, chunky cucumbers is delightful. Use them sliced on top of hard, nutty-tasting cheeses in sandwiches made of rye bread with caraway seeds, or as a scoop for soft rich cream cheese. You will need clip-top 'parfait' jars or screw-top preserving jars: wash and sterilize them either by boiling them in water for 10 minutes or baking them in the oven for 30 minutes. Alternatively, use a rigid plastic container with a close-fitting lid. I have also been reliably informed that a dishwasher can sterilize equipment, too, by using the hottest setting.

Makes 5 kg
- 10 litres bottled spring water
- 500 g coarse-textured organic sea salt
- 4 × 5-cm pieces fresh root ginger
- 6 red pickling peppers (mild chilli peppers)
- 6 cloves garlic, peeled
- 1 level tablespoon mixed pickling spice
- 6 fresh bay leaves
- sprigs of fresh or dried dill flowers
- 2 teaspoons acetic acid or white wine vinegar
- 5 kg firm green pickling cucumbers, 15 cm long, without marks or blemishes – they are more readily available in early autumn

Put the water into a preserving pan and add the salt and all the other ingredients except the cucumbers. Bring it to the boil, stirring until the salt has dissolved, and boil rapidly for 5 minutes. Take it off the heat and leave it until it is cold. Meanwhile, scrub the cucumbers thoroughly with a small bristle nailbrush (keep one for the kitchen rather than using the bathroom one). Rinse them in cold water, then commence filling a plastic or enamel bucket to within 5 cm of the top with the cucumbers. First, strain the pickling liquid, reserving the spices. Put a layer of cucumber into the bucket, and scatter over some of the reserved spices. Continue until all the cucumbers are in the bucket: they should come to 5 cm below the top. Cover the cucumbers with a large, upturned plate, then weight it with a clean brick sealed in a plastic bag. Carefully pour the cold pickling solution in a trickle down the side of the bucket until it covers the plate to the depth of 2.5 cm. Cover with a muslin cloth or thin tea-towel, and leave in a cool place, such as a garage, toolshed or unheated spare room, for 10 days. After 10 days, skim off the froth that will have appeared on the surface. Cover and leave for a further week. Skim again, and test by slicing into a cucumber. If the taste is not right, leave them for a further week, or until they are ready (the speed of the pickle in acquiring the sharp, tangy taste depends on the temperature around them). When the cucumbers are ready, skim them again, pack them into the large plastic containers or the glass jars and fill with the pickling liquid until the cucumbers are submerged. Store in the refrigerator.

Note: This is rather laborious isn't it? But I can assure you it's well worth it if you love pickles, and in fact I know it's one recipe that men reluctant to venture into the kitchen find they can prepare successfully.

HAPPINESS IS A HARD BIT OF DRIED-OUT CHEESE

'I've just found a piece of dried-out cheese lurking in the back of my fridge,' wailed an anguished customer over the phone one day. 'What am I supposed to do with it now? Should I chuck it out?'

'No way,' came back my horrified reply. 'There are all sorts of ways to put dry cheese to good use.'

Finding bits of dry cheese can be annoying: you hate to be wasteful, yet you're not sure what to do with it. If it is goat's cheese, the taste will not be affected as it will have become crumblier and sweeter. When you grate it over pasta, or mix it into a risotto or salad, it tastes gentle and mellow. A cow's milk hard cheese past its best can be finely grated and mixed with grated Parmigiano to top pasta or risotto. It is only the soft white-crust cheeses, such as Brie, that lose their charm when they've hardened. You have to bite the bullet and throw them out. The moral of the story is to buy little and often, rather than a big lump for the week.

Here are a few ideas for using up a bit of leftover cheese, or combining a few bits and pieces together.

Dry goat's cheeses can be grated finely or shaved into curls and placed on toasted bread, brushed with an aromatized oil (infused with, say, chilli, or sweet dried peppers, or herbs, or lemon zest). Add roasted baby vine tomatoes, or peppers, for an easy lunch or supper snack. Scramble eggs in the usual way; add freshly ground black pepper and a little coarse organic sea salt, Piadina bread (see page 37) or similar simple country-style bread alongside and you have a great late breakfast.

Make an improvised savoury tarte tatin with some bread that seems a little stale: dry out thickly sliced bread in the oven and top it with thin slices of semi-hard fruity cheeses that no longer look good on the cheeseboard as they've been chopped about a bit. Peel and slice good dessert apples, refresh them in acidulated water to stop them going brown, pat them dry and fry them in butter until golden. Place on top of the cheese, sprinkle over a little sugar and finely chopped thyme, then flash under the grill to bubble up the cheese and caramelize the apples.

Experiment with pears and cream cheese, or slowly braise onions with olive oil, adding a little balsamic vinegar, to serve alongside Piadina or other country-style bread (see page 37) with grated cheeses melted on top.

Slice some underripe or green tomatoes, dip them in egg and coat generously in finely grated cheese, then fry in olive oil until golden. Serve with pan-fried salame.

Finely grated cheese mixed with chopped fresh herbs can be used to coat fish, chicken breasts, or rack of lamb, before roasting, frying or grilling.

If you hate to throw away the hard rind of Parmigiano Reggiano or Grana di Padano, why not grind it finely in a food-processor and mix in extra-virgin olive oil to make a smooth paste? Store in a preserving jar or other container with a tight-fitting lid and keep in the bottom of the fridge. You can use the paste to coat pasta, or mix into a well-flavoured and reduced tomato sauce, or as a base for a salad dressing. I've even tried it beaten into puréed potatoes.

Here's an extract from a fax I sent to a chef who had found some leftover buffalo ricotta in his fridge.

There is a way of using fresh cheese or soft cheese in Lyon, in France, called *Cervelle de Canut* or *Claqueret Lyonnais*. Pass the cheese through a sieve and mix in finely ground pepper, salt, minced shallot, herbs, such as chives, flat parsley, maybe basil, marjoram (aromatic herbs) finely chopped, minced fresh garlic. Place in an earthenware pot, cover and keep cold for a day or so to let the flavours infuse. Then pour the following over the cheese but don't stir it in, just let it lie over the top: a mixture of good olive oil, fruity light white wine and good-quality white wine vinegar. Leave for another day to ripen in the fridge. Serve with bread to scoop up the cheese mixture, and perhaps make a salsa with minced Taggiasche olives, capers and flat-leaf parsley. Make a dressing with extra-virgin olive oil, balsamic vinegar, and aromatic herbs, such as rosemary, thyme and tarragon, and pour over the olive mixture. Heap a little alongside the cheese.

If as it's 8 days old the cheese is too acidic, try mellowing it with a little mascarpone or light cream.

Another idea – if you can get hold of fresh vine leaves from the Farmers' Market or from your greengrocer, wrap the ricotta (mixed with herbs if you wish or just with a little pepper) and tie it up with fine string, if necessary. Then brush lightly with olive oil and bake in the embers of your woodburning oven. Or place the vine-wrapped cheeses closely together in an ovenproof dish with some tomato sauce, which has been slow cooked and thickened considerably, drizzle over some olive oil and bake slowly. Or shape the strained cheese into slightly flattened balls, wrap in thin slices of *pancetta* and bake or skewer them on bamboo sticks (previously soaked in water) before barbecuing.

Stuff the curd, mixed with herbs including fennel or dill, into fish before baking.

Make the curd into fresh 'quenelles' and serve in soup, maybe?

Hope this gives you some ideas . . . all the best!

EPILOGUE

Let me end this book with a little bit of irony. I've just had a phone call from my old friend John, who thinks I'm sometimes too serious when it comes to discussing food. Anyway, he tells me that he went out to do a little food shopping and had the urge to buy some Dairylea processed cheese, and what did I have to say about that?

'Oh, wonderful,' I replied. 'Do what I do and get some Heinz spaghetti – not the hoops. When the spag's hot, put it in a bowl and dot lots of bits of the Dairylea over the top then flash it under a really hot grill until it's all bubbling.'

'You're kidding me,' he replied, suitably taken aback.

'Nope, it's a fave, especially on stressful days and extremely happy days. Try it some time.'

And there's lots more where that came from – my girls will attest to toasted white thick-sliced bread lightly buttered, then spread with Marmite, before Cheddar of the highest quality, such as Montgomery's, is generously shredded over the top then shoved under the hot grill to bubble and toast the cheese to a golden crunchiness. We can love cheese in many different ways – so go out there and experiment.

POSTSCRIPT

BEAUTY TIP

Who would have thought a book on cheese would contain a beauty tip? Not such a daft idea, as we should all know about the health-enhancing qualities of cheese – good for teeth and bones as well as the blessed dietary attributes of Parmigiano Reggiano for young children, women in pregnancy, the elderly and the sporty types. However, both my daughters are complimented time and again on their flowing locks and strong, beautifully manicured nails. How do they do it? What is their secret? Both Kate and Rose, without hesitation or prompting by me, say it's because of their consumption of good cheese and yoghurt throughout their life, and without my considerable consumption, too, during both pregnancies. I may be prejudiced in thinking I have two absolutely gorgeous daughters, but I just have to look at their silky hair and strong nails, their perfect complexion and trouble-free toothy smiles, and if that's not a good advertisement for cheese, then I don't know what is!

GOOD CHEESE SHOPS

If you don't see one listed that is near you, telephone the Specialist Cheesemakers Association in London on 020 7253 2114, or Juliet Harbutt at British Cheese Awards on 01608 650325. Also, search out weekly Farmers' Markets – you will find information about them in local newspapers or tourist information centres.

ENGLAND, SCOTLAND AND WALES

Abergavenny: Abergavenny Fine Foods, Unit 4, Castle Meadow Park, Abergavenny, Gwent NR7 7RZ. Tel: 01873 850001 (contact them for Welsh cheeses)

Bath: Fine Cheese Co., 29 Walcot Street, Bath BA1 5BN

Beckenham: James's, 188 High Street, Beckenham, Kent BR3 1EN (some cheeses ageing on site)

Brighton: The Cheese Shop, 17 Kensington Gardens, Brighton, West Sussex BN1 4AL

Chester: The Cheese Shop, 118 Northgate Street, Chester CH1 2HT (some cheeses ageing on site)

Clevedon: The Olive Garden, 87a Hill Road, Clevedon, North Somerset BS21 7PN

Edinburgh: Ian Mellis, Cheesemonger, 30a Victoria Street, Edinburgh EH1 2JN (matures on site with special emphasis on Scottish farmhouse cheeses)

—— Valvona & Crolla, 19 Elm Row, Edinburgh EH7 4AA

Herstmonceaux: Say Cheese, Gardner Street, Herstmonceux, East Sussex BN27 4LE (good display of local cheeses)

Iwerne Minster: Harvell the Butcher Shop, Iwerne Minster, Dorset

Kendal: Peter Gott at Sillfield Farm, Edmoor, Kendal, Cumbria. Tel: 01539 587328 – call for details of outlets and markets

London: Brindisa at Borough Market, London Bridge, London SE1 (Spanish cheese specialist)

——Cheeseboard, 26 Royal Hill, Greenwich, London SE10 8RT

——Cheeses, Fortis Green Road, Muswell Hill, London N10

——Clarke's, 122 Kensington Church Street, London W8 4BH (selected Neal's Yard and La Fromagerie cheeses)

——La Fromagerie, 30 Highbury Park, London N5 2AA (cheeses maturing on site. French, Italian and British cheeses from traditional cheesemakers)

——Jeroboam's, 51 Elizabeth Street, London SW1W 9PP

——Neal's Yard Dairy, 17 Shorts Gardens, London WC2H 9AT (matures on site, the major player in British cheese)

——Paxton & Whitfield, 93 Jermyn Street, London W1

——Villandry, Great Portland Street, London W1

Manchester: Cheese Hamlet, 706 Wilmslow Road, Didsbury, Manchester M20 0DW

Marlborough: Mackintosh of Marlborough, 42a High Street, Marlborough, Wiltshire SN8 1HQ

Oxford: Oxford Cheese Company, 17 Covered Market, Oxford OX1 1EF

Shrewsbury: Appleyards, 86 Wyle Cop, Shrewsbury, Shropshire SY1 1UT

Totnes: Ticklemore Cheeses, 1 Ticklemore Street, Totnes, Devon TQ9 5EJ (cheesemakers and shop)

IRELAND

Dublin: Sheridan's Cheesemongers, 11 South Anne Street, Dublin 2 (for Irish farmhouse cheeses)

Galway: McCambridge's, 38–9 Shop Street, Galway

FRANCE

Aix-en-Provence: Gérard Paul, 9 rue des Marseillais, 13100
  Aix-en-Provence
Alsace: Jacky Quesnot, Fromagerie Saint-Nicolas, 18 rue Saint-Nicolas,
  88000 Colmar, Haut Rhin
Boulogne-sur-Mer: Philippe Olivier, 43–5 rue Thiers, Boulogne-sur-Mer
Cannes: Edouard Céneri, La Ferme Savoyarde, 22 rue Meynier, 06400
  Cannes
Chambéry: Denis Provent, Laiterie des Halles, 2 Place de Genève, 73000
  Chambéry
Lyon: Maréchal, Halles de Lyon, 102 Cours Lafayette, 69003 Lyon
—— Renée & René Richard, Halles de Lyon, 102 Courts Lafayette,
  69003 Lyon
Paris: Alleosse, 13 rue Poncelet, 75017 Paris (visit the shop on Sunday to
  experience the most sophisticated open-air market too)
—— Pierre Androuet, 41 rue d'Amsterdam, 75008 Paris
—— Roland Barthélémy, 51 rue de Grenelle, 75007 Paris
—— Marie-Anne Cantin, 12 rue de Champ-de-Mars, 75007 Paris
—— La Ferme Saint-Aubin, 76 rue Saint-Louis-en-l'Île, 75004 Paris
—— La Fromagerie Boursault, 71 avenue du Général Leclerc, 75014 Paris
Pau: Gabriel Bachelet, 24 rue du Maréchal-Joffre, Pau 64000
Roquefort-sur-Soulzon: Gabriel Coulet, Le Papillon, Société des Caves,
  12250 Roquefort-sur-Soulzon (visit Roquefort caves)
Thonon-les-Bains: Daniel Boujon, 7 rue Saint-Sébastien, 74200
  Thonon-les-Bains
Toulouse: Xavier Bourgon, 6 place Victor-Hugo, 31000 Toulouse

ITALY

There are covered markets in every town and city, and open-air ones too.
These are well worth visiting, but get there early as they usually close by
lunchtime.

Bologna: Salsamenteria Taburini, via Caprarie 1, Bologna (famed for ham and Parmigiano Reggiano)

Cuneo: Cucina del Cornale, 12050 Maglaino Alfieri (a co-operative for local organic farmers to sell their produce)

Milan: Casa del Formaggio, via Speronari 3, Milan

——Peck, via Spadari 9, Milan (an institution as well as the most stunning display of produce)

Rome: Bucci Alimentari, via Flaminia 44, Rome (but also find out about the local markets)

PORTUGAL

Portuguesefoods.com, tel/fax: 0044 207 737 7313

Tim Clements searches out artisan-made cheese and produce, and manufactures Elvas plums. He has a London base.

SPAIN

Barcelona: Tutusaus, tel: 93209 8373, specialists in farmhouse cheeses; the owner, Isabelle, speaks English

CYPRUS

Nicosia: Il Paesano, 31 Byzantiou 8, 10 Zinonos Kitleos, 2064 Strovolos, Nicosia

AUSTRALIA

Melbourne: Richmond Hill Café & Larder, Melbourne (Will Studd has his cheeses for sale here and is the founder of the Australian Cheese Society)

Brisbane: Kelly's on Zillman, PO Box 22, Underwood, Queensland 4119
(cheese importer and judge: John McDonald, e-mail:
johnmcd@gil.com.au)

NEW ZEALAND

Auckland: Vinotica Products Ltd, Unit D3, Henry Rose Place, Albany,
1331 Auckland

USA

Ann Arbor: Ari Weinzweig, Zingeman's Delicatessen, 422 Detroit
Street, Ann Arbor, MI 48184 (leading voice of the American Cheese
Society)
New York City: Murray's Cheeses on Bleecker Street and Artisan on
Park Avenue
San Francisco: Tomales Bay Cheeses, Tomales Bay

COOKWARE BY MAIL ORDER

Hampshire Cookware and Catering Supplies Ltd, tel: 02392 324555,
website: www.hantscook.co.uk, e-mail: info@hantscook.co.uk
Mermaid. Tel: (0044) 0121 507 8844, e-mail: sales@mermaidcookware.com

BIBLIOGRAPHY

Some books that have been of help and comfort to me:

Androuet, Pierre, *Guide to Cheeses*, Paris, Editions Stock, 1983
Carroll, Ricki, and Robert Carroll, *Cheesemaking Made Easy*, Vermont, Storey Communications Inc., 1996
Ciletti, Barbara, *Making Great Cheese*, North Carolina, Lark Books, 1999
Coffe, Jean-Pierre, *A Vos Paniers*, Paris, Guides Balland, 1993
Courtine, Robert J., *Larousse des Fromages*, Paris, Courtine, 1990
Fiori, Giacomo, *Formaggi Italiani*, Verolengo, EOS Editrice, 2000
Jenkins, Steven, *The Cheese Primer*, New York, Workman Publishing, 1996
Rance, Patrick, *The Great British Cheese Book*, London, Macmillan, 1988
Rance, Patrick, *French Cheese*, London, Macmillan, 1989
Studd, Will, *Chalk and Cheese*, Australia, Purple Egg Publishers, 1999
Warlin, Laura, *The New American Cheese*, New York, Stewart, Tabori Chang, 2000

Books I keep close at hand:

All of Elizabeth David's oeuvre
Andries de Groot, Roy, *The Auberge of the Flowering Hearth*, New York, Ecco Press, 1983
Behr, Edward, *The Art of Eating* (quarterly magazine: telephone: 001 802 592 3411, or fax: 001 802 592 3400; website: www.artofeating.com)
Berger, John, *Pig Earth*, London, Bloomsbury, 1979
Graham, Peter, *Mourjou, The Life and Food of an Auvergne Village*, Harmondsworth, Penguin, 1998

Plotkin, Fred, *Italy for the Gourmet Traveller*, London, Kyle Cathie, 1996

Wells, Patricia, *The Food Lover's Guide to France*, London, Methuen, 1984

Whiting, John, *Through Darkest Gaul*, London, Diatribal Press, 1997

ACKNOWLEDGEMENTS

First I must thank all at Penguin for producing this book, but especially Lindsey Jordan who took my idea from the outset, and let me 'fly', allowing my voice to be heard; Hazel Orme, my copy-editor, who corrected and somehow managed to make sense of everything; Craig for the wonderful layout; Ed for the stunning jacket; and Tatiana for the special photography showing us in a natural way, and giving the pictures a truth and purity. I have enjoyed every minute spent writing this book and am indebted to a wonderful publishing team.

There is a saying, 'It's those behind more gratulate', that says it all for me. My shop comes alive with all the wonderful produce from dedicated, inspired people. If you don't see your name you know who you are because I love you all and respect you enormously.

First I must thank my husband Danny, who not only works alongside me but also has to come home and live with me too. Then there is my very special colleague Eric Demelle, who is the heartbeat of the Cheese Room. His depth of knowledge, and sheer love of all things cheese, has helped make La Fromagerie such an individual and exciting business. Also the fact that he is a big fan of Johnny Hallyday helps too. I have a great team of assistants in the shop and their enthusiasm and good humour make every day a pleasure. We work very hard, but we have fun too.

I couldn't not mention Laurent, who trucks in produce from France, and has known me since I started working from home, when he manoeuvred his lorry down a narrow Highgate street, causing a few net curtains to twitch nervously in the process.

A big cheer and heartfelt thanks to all the artisan cheesemakers wherever you may be. Never give up, and always strive for perfection. Let's not lose individuality and respect for tradition; the enjoyment of nature's gift should never be compromised.

In France I have to embrace warmly, and thank profusely, Gabriel Bachelet, Xavier Bourgon, Denis Provent, Philippe Olivier, and myriad suppliers and cheesemakers; I am in awe and indebted to them all, and hope our future is secure for many years to come.

With special thanks to my Italian master of cheese, Dottore Carlo Fiori, who has tirelessly provided me with artisan cheeses and is always open to suggestions (on cheese matters).

With extra special thanks to Geoff Owen, who has driven me round Italy and I have driven him round the bend with my requests. His patience, enthusiasm, and shared curiosity on food matters, as well as his bloody hard work, have given my business the edge on artisan-made goods from Italy, and some of the more individual styles of wines.

And thanks, too, to all the chefs, food writers, food campaigners and especially good friends like Nigel Slater, Jamie Oliver and Hugo Arnold who share my passion for food, as well as all the lovely people we supply in the restaurant and wholesale side of the business. Also Klaus and Colin for making all the *traiteur* food items that make such an impact in the front of the shop, and all the bakers still prepared to work tirelessly by hand-producing real-tasting breads.

I give my daughters Kate and Rose a big kiss and a hug for encouraging me first to start my own business and then to keep on going even when I felt like giving up through sheer exhaustion. And Patch for waiting up for me even when I get home in the early hours.

And finally a big thank you to all the people who visit my shop, and chat and have become part of my ever extending 'family'. Nothing gives me more pleasure than seeing you all taste and enjoy our produce.

INDEX